Sports, Recreation,

Table of Contents

Introduction 1

Songs 4

Sports Activities 4

Games & Activities 5

Crafts 36

Fine & Performing Arts Signs 50

Sports & Recreation Signs 82

Handouts 136

Index 142

Introducing Basic Creative Drama Skills

Creative drama involves skill building. After preliminary work has been undertaken in forming rapport with the group, establishing a creative climate, and warming up the players so that they feel more relaxed and confident, the leader will want to introduce slightly more difficult activities such as those that deal with concentration, visualization, social interaction, and physicalization. When they are not easily distracted and have confidence in their vocal and physical proficiency, players are likely to create more believable characterizations and to experience stronger empathetic responses. Most leaders find that complex activities are played more successfully when a solid foundation of basic skills has been laid. In order to help participants realize their abilities in these areas, the leader should use early sessions to introduce activities designed to facilitate skill development. These can be reintroduced and replayed in future sessions, even if these later sessions are more complex in nature. Each time these skill building activities are done, players should demonstrate increased self assurance and greater depth of involvement. As security in and knowledge of basic dramatic skills grows, they should display more imaginative responses, demonstrate increased emotional sensitivity to the materials, and become more attuned to the creative ideas of their fellow peers.

Drama Performance Tips

1. Resist the urge to unconsciously unbutton or unzip or otherwise fiddle with your clothes while performing: it is distracting to the audience.
2. Set your feet, one slightly in front of the other, to avoid shifting from foot to foot unconsciously, moving your feet back and forth, or rocking your body.
3. Keep your body at a 45-degree angle, so that the entire audience can see most of you all the time. When you play two characters in a dialogue scene, face one character in a 45-degree angle one way, and then face the other way at a 45-degree angle when playing the second character. This also avoids the annoying phrases "he said" and "she said" whenever a character speaks in the scene. We know by position which character is speaking in that scene.
4. Pan so that you have eye contact with all your audience. Remember to have eye contact with those near you as well as those in the back. For those who feel uncomfortable looking at the audience directly, pick a spot above the audience's heads and pan using this spot. Don't look down at the floor. The floor stops your voice and the floor is not listening to you.
5. If the conclusion of your story doesn't feel right to you, change the ending so it does. It's your story to tell!
6. Whatever your character is doing and feeling at a particular moment in your story, your face, body, hand gestures, dialogue, vocal tone and pitch, and word choice should all focus on bringing that moment to life for your listeners. Show the audience; don't have the characters report to them.
7. Do not wear a hat or allow your hair to cover or shadow your face so that the audience can't see your facial expressions clearly. Do not wear sleeves that hang over your hands or flap; such sleeves hide your hand gestures and the flapping distracts listeners from what you're saying. Don't wear hanging, clanging, or swinging jewelry that distracts the audience, or that temps you to play with it while you're performing.

8. Avoid laughing or giggling at what you're doing: it makes your listeners feel you're not sincere and that you don't believe in the story you're sharing.
9. If characters or objects in your story are different sizes or at different heights, look up when you're lower and down when you're higher.
10. Keep your hands at your sides or in front of you when not gesturing. Keep your hands out of your pockets. Don't lock your fingers together in front of you or play with your fingers.
11. Be careful not to swallow or mumble the ends of sentences, or rush through your narrative part. Try to keep your voice toward the top of your throat. Think of arching your speaking voice up to the cavity near the top of your head.
12. Take a moment before you begin telling to your audience: inhale and exhale a few deep breaths to relax and open your throat.
13. Wait to begin speaking until you're on the stage in front of the audience. Don't begin talking as you're walking on stage unless you've designed your performance that way for a special reason.
14. Keep the words you use appropriate to the time and culture of the story you're telling. For example "Give me a break!" and "Hang in there!" are not suitable dialogue when you're telling "Ali Babba and the Forty Thieves."
15. If your story comes from a different culture—with some unusual words or character names or interesting concepts your listeners should know about—take time to introduce these or explain before you begin to tell your tale. In this way, your listeners will be prepared, can enjoy your story, and won't have to wonder what something means.
16. Begin your story with high but controlled energy. Step into the telling! This doesn't mean you should speed up your telling, but rather be completely focused on the story and connected with the audience. You can feel it when you're at this level.
17. Nervous? Every performer who goes before an audience should be nervous. A performer needs this nervous energy to gear up to "step into" the presentation. A confident, seasoned performer, one who knows the tales and how he or she wants to perform, controls this nervousness to focus the energy and improve the performance. An inexperienced performer may be so controlled by nervousness that he or she doesn't perform well.
18. Many stories have repeating phrases, ideas, and situations. For these it is usually more effective to repeat them in a different way by changing the emphases, your tone and emotion, pacing, or phrasing. This is especially so in the "add-on" stories—for example, in which the dog asks the cat who asks the water who asks the skunk…
19. A story is normally told in the past tense: the action has already happened. So the narrator should say, "John said," not "John says."
20. If you're portraying an animal or creature, then try to become that animal as much as possible. If you're a turtle, then move your head, neck, legs, and arms like a turtle would move.
21. Keep visible at all times. Don't get down on the floor to act out a role if your audience will not be able to see you.
22. Don't keep repeating "You know" over and over. Your audience didn't come to listen to what they already "know."

Copyright © 2005 Time to Sign, Inc.

Sports, Recreation, & Arts

23. Don't wave your hands around. Keep your arms and hands at your sides until you clearly need them to make a gesture that brings your character to life at that moment. Gestures should support your story, not distract from it.
24. A story should be entertaining. You and your audience should enjoy sharing a tale well told. It's a group experience, and you are part of the group.

Pantomime

Pantomime is the expression of thoughts, feelings, and actions through physical means. Players use the bodies, but not sound, to communicate. When players begin working on more complex materials, they realize the value of being able to portray a character vocally and physically. In the early stages of drama, however, some are overwhelmed by the thought of speaking and doing simultaneously. Still others are concerned with developing physical coordination and precision. These factors support an early focus of pantomime. Players should feel comfortable knowing that physical portrayals are clear and accurate before they undertake the creation of dialogue. Paying attention to surroundings, human behavior, and interactions is fundamental for sharpening pantomime skills. In helping players to develop these skills, the leader should note the value of observation (the ability to see clearly and to note details), sensory awareness (seeing, hearing, tasting, feeling, and smelling), and imagination (engagement of the mind's eye in creative thought, picturization, or fanciful depictions). Concentration is also necessary to convey experiences successfully through physical action. The goal should be image recognition, not stumping those watching nor producing a guessing game. An image, however, cannot be effectively conveyed through pantomime if it is not clear in the player's own mind. Action and emotional responses drive pantomime materials and these should always be created using active, rather than passive, verbs. It is much more stimulating to begin with, "Show me how you look when…" or, "you are…" than with, "be a…" The latter tends toward introspection generating little action. Having something to do or show clearly keeps players better focused and making active choices.

Types of Tales

Folktale: Tale from the oral tradition that has been handed down through generations and from place to place, with characters and scenes changing according to locations. These oral tales include myths, legends, fairy tales, fables, and tall tales. They usually portray people suddenly thrust into extraordinary times and situations.
Myth: Usually explains why something is the way it is such as why the sea is salty or why the sun is in the sky. Most myths involve gods or religion.
Fairy Tales: A story that involves magic, usually through the powers of some magical figure such as an elf, fairy, gnome, witch, godmother, sorcerer, or genie.
Legend: A story told about a historical place, person, or event, with a small bit of fact or truth in it. The storyteller embellishes and exaggerates the fact or truth in the telling.
Tall Tales: A wild, exaggerated tale about people or events told as if it were true. Many American tall tales—Paul Bunyan, Joe Magarac, John Henry—are stories manufactured by industry so the workers will work harder and produce more, becoming that industry's heroes.

Fable: A story that teaches a lesson or moral, focusing on the listener's ability to reason, understand, and learn the lesson or moral. With a fable, the listener doesn't become emotionally involved. Therefore, many fables use animal characters with which the listener cannot identify as representing him or her.
Literary Tales: A story created and written by an author as if it were a folktale. Such authors include Hans Christian Anderson, Edgar Allen Poe, Mark Twain, and O. Henry.
Epic or Saga: Usually told in poetry form, it features a hero, such as Robin Hood, Beowulf, or King Arthur, who has a series of adventures.
Griot: An African who sings songs, tells stories, and recounts the history of his or her native land.

Story Teller Telling Tips

As a storyteller, you continually learn, grow, and change along with your tales. The following is a list of skills to improve story telling:

- **Vocal projections:** Can you be heard by everyone?
- **Clarity:** Is your speech clear and understandable?
- **Pacing:** Do you speak at a pace that's easy for the listeners to follow, but not so slow that the story drags?
- **Characters:** Do you show the character through action and give some description of the character?
- **Dialogue:** Do you bring the characters to life by having them speak?
- **Words to avoid:** Do you avoid slang terms, "ums," "aahs," repeated "ands" that string sentences together, "you knows," and "he went" rather than "he said"?
- **Preparation:** Do you know your story so well that there's no chance of forgetting it?
- **Dramatic gestures:** Do you use your hands, eyes, face, and body to bring the characters and actions to life?
- **Intensity:** When you tell, do you hold your audience's interest? Does it feel as if there were a wall around you and your audience, and that you've moved into another world, another dimension?

Songs

The Camping Song

Did You Ever Go A Camping

It's Summer time Again

Sports Activities

Baseball
Basketball
Bicycling
Boating
Camping
Cheering
Climbing
Fishing

Sports, Recreation, & Arts

Football
Golf
Gymnastics
Horseback Riding
Ice Skating
Olympics
Skateboarding
Soccer
Swimming
Tennis
Track & Field
Volleyball

Games and Activities

Airplane Scale (sports & recreation)

This balance skill is performed on one foot. The student raises one leg behind them and leans forward. Their arms should be spread out to the sides. This position will resemble an airplane. Hold this balance for ten seconds. You will be surprised how difficult it is to hold this position without moving and losing balance.

Topical signs to be learned: airplane, skill, look, like, numbers 1-10, don't move.

The Alphabet Game (fine & performing arts, language arts)

With a scene partner (or a group), choose a who, what, and where. The first line of your scene must start with the letter A. The second line of your scene must start with the letter B, and so on throughout the alphabet. As you improvise your scene, each line must start with the next letter of the alphabet. If you have trouble remembering where you are, and if you have a third player, you can have him call out the next letter after each line of dialogue. Your scene should end when you get to the letter Z.

Topical signs to be learned: alphabet signs, who, what, where, begin.

Back Roll (sports & recreation)

Equipment: mats

Here's how to perform a back roll. From a standing start, sit down and tuck the body into a tight ball. Roll backwards with the hands placed on either side of the head. When the hands come in contact with the mats, push downwards. The hands will continue to be pushed downward as the feet are swung around to contact the floor. Watch out for your students trying to "throw" their backs backwards. This will cause them to land with a hard "thump" on the mat. The back needs to remain in a tight tuck as the student rolls backwards to his hands.

Topical signs to be learned: tight, roll, stand, sit, ball, hands.

Ball Conversation (sports & recreation)

Materials: balls for every child or every two children (optional)

Players take turns "bouncing" rhythmic messages to one another in a conversational style. One player improvises a pattern which is echoed by the second player. Then, both players are encouraged to improvise original patterns. For younger players, each should be furnished with a ball for conversations that ""flow" well. With older players, one ball may be passed between the two children.

Topical signs to be learned: ball, bounce, both, pass.

Balloon Volleyball (sports & recreation)

Equipment: rope or clothesline, balloons.

Clear a playing court, and the area around it. Place a length of rope or clothesline across the floor in the middle of the room to indicate sides. Blow up a balloon to use as a volleyball. Then divide into two teams and swat the balloon back and forth across the line. A team gets a point if the balloon hits the floor on the opponent's side or if an opponent fails to hit it back over the string to the opposite side in three tries. For a livelier game, inflate two balloons of different colors and play with both at once. One team gets a point each time the first balloon hits the floor on the opponent's side; the other team scores with the other balloon.

Topical signs to be learned: balloon, volleyball, team, across, line, touch, try, three.

Blob (sports & recreation)

This game can have 10-50+ players. The name of this game was derived from the movie "The Blob." In playing the game, we can pretend that a UFO has landed in our town and, just like in the movie, some kind of gooey alien has started catching people and turning them into blobs. And, also like in the movie, when a blob gets to be a certain size, it splits into two blobs. In this game, however, the human race loses as everyone becomes a blob. Oh, well.

What actually happens in the game is that, after defining the play area, we somehow find someone to be our initial blob. Then that person must, within the defined boundaries, catch another person by tagging. They then link by holding hands and can catch someone only while being linked. When they catch someone, the third person links with them as well. Only the outside hand on either end of the blob can tag players. However, when a fourth person is caught, something special happens: mitosis! For non-biologists, it means the blob divides in two. Now two blobs stalk humans. Each time there are four in a blob, they can divide again. After a while, there is nowhere a poor human can go to escape. What fun! Reminds players to be aware of each other to avoid crashing into on another.

Topical signs to be learned: game, divide/separate, catch.

Sports, Recreation, & Arts

Body Sculptures (sports & recreation)
Players construct body sculptures of victory, defeat, excitement, suspense, and disappointment. Any number of players can contribute to each sculpture.

Topical signs to be learned: body, sculpture (statue), win, lose, excited, other sports signs.

Capture the Flag (sports & recreation)
Materials: whistle, arm bands (gauze or different colored fabric), flag for each team, moveable flag pole (optional).

Divide the teams as evenly as possible. The division line and outer boundaries should be clearly explained to all the players. The size should be determined by terrain, time of day and amount of playing time. Usually the size should be a football field or larger. Give each player an armband to tie somewhere between the wrist and shoulder. If you have all one color arm bands one team can have one team wear them on the left and the other on the right. These bands cannot be covered with clothing nor changed from one arm to another.

When all the bands have been given out, each team takes its flag and places it somewhere within its own territory. After 10 minutes a whistle or bugle blows and the game starts. The first team to bring the opponents' flag to the game leader wins the game. Some from each time try to capture the opponents' flag; others try to defend their flag. A person is "killed" by having his arm band torn off. A person may play only when he has his arm band on. When it is torn off, he must go back to the leader and obtain a new band. Or each side can have a "prison" in their territory where they may place opponents captured in their territory only. A team member can release the "prisoners" by tagging them.

Special Rules:
In fighting, there must be no dirty play (e.g. slugging, kicking).
The flag may be moved during the game.
No one may use an arm band taken from another person. He must get a new one.
No one is allowed in or under any building or shelter or in any tree.
Anyone going out of bounds must forfeit his arm band.
Announce the game's end by a loud blast of a whistle or bugle.

Topical signs to be learned: flag, catch, take, team, whistle, start, finish, line.

Chain Stories (fine & performing arts)
Have the group sit in a circle or in concentric circles, or if only two people are playing sit across from each other. One person says a word, then the next person adds a word, until there's a complete sentence. Try not to pause. There are no wrong answers in this game. Just say the first word that pops into your head and see if the story makes sense. It's ok if the person after you doesn't say what you thought they would say. It's okay if you're not sure what the person before you is thinking. Continue until some type of story emerges. Perhaps stop for a moment to ask what has happened so far, or what some think may happen next. Then continue

adding words and sentences together. The next step could be the one-sentence chain story. Each person adds a sentence to whatever came before in the circle. Or you can play One Word Story Ball. Instead of telling the story in a circle, toss a ball to someone as you say one word. They say the next word in a sentence as they toss the ball to someone else, and so on.

Advanced Version
The chained story becomes a timed tale. Each person in the circle speaks for one or two minutes. Even if someone pauses or doesn't know what to say next, everyone waits until that person's time is up. (It's amazing just how long one minute can seem!)

If you are sitting in concentric circles, the inner circle of people might tell the tale. After they are done, the outer circle of people might summarize what they heard as well as what hindered the story from being better and how the telling might improve. (Often, those telling the story begin to repeat the same incidents over and over: actions are just strung together with little embellishment; there's little character, background, or scene detail; and very little dialogue has been included.) Now that the group knows some ways to improve a story-telling, start another chain story focusing on these ingredients. The outer group becomes the inner one and does the telling this time. Afterward, evaluate the story again. See how the telling as improved and what still could be developed. After all, a story—especially an oral one—is always in the process of developing, evolving, in need of revision—a good thing for young people to understand and learn.

Topical signs to be learned: sit in circle, say, tell, continue, word, add, story, what happened, next, sentence.

Character Letters as Reader's Theatre (fine & performing arts)
Materials: folktales, paper, pen or pencil.

Choose a folktale. Then choose one person to represent each main character in the story. Each person writes a letter telling what happened in the story form his or her character's point of view. The letter should capture the feelings, language, and views of that character. Stage a reader's theatre with each person reading his or her character's letter. A narrator might begin the story, or summarize the story and introduce each character, who then reads the letter. If there are too many students to participate in one folktale, then do several folktales. The group might try writing the letter in a mysterious language. The person who has written the letter keeps a description of what was actually written. This isn't revealed to the performers until they perform what they think the letter means. The letter writer or reader can clue the performers through voice inflection and emotion.

Topical signs to be learned: character, story, write, letter, emotion signs, narrator.

Characters of the Space (fine & performing arts)
An actor should always be familiar with the space in which he or she is acting. This activity helps you get to know your space, as well as warm up your body, and practice using your body in different ways.

Sports, Recreation, & Arts   9

Walk around in the space you're in. Keep walking, only now you're pretending you're walking through pudding. Think about what it feels like and how your body would move through pudding. For example, you might move more slowly because pudding is thicker than air. After a while, pretend the space has turned into clouds. Think about what that feels like, and how you might walk through clouds. The space can turn into all sorts of things. Someone is appointed the caller and whenever she calls out, it will change the way you move.

Suggestions for different kinds of spaces: honey, snow, water, mashed potatoes, outer space, popcorn, wind, feathers, mud, fire, taffy, pea soup, tar.

Shoe Character of the Space
Pretend you have on different kinds of shoes. Whenever a new shoe is called, it will change the way you move.
Suggestions for different kinds of shoes: roller skates, space boots, moccasins, ballet slippers, ice skates, tap shoes, tennis shoes, cowboy boots, cleats, motorcycle boots, high heels, platforms, clogs, army boots.

Topical signs to be learned: walk, through, way, pretend, think, feel, move, change, shoes.

Concentration Activity: I'm Going to the Game (sports & recreation)
Players build a list by naming items they would take to a game. Each player must name all the things the previous players have said and then add an item.

Example: Leader: I'm going to the game and I'm going to take binoculars.
Player 1: I'm going to the game and I'm going to take binoculars and a seat cushion.

You can play this for any type of activity or outing such as going on vacation, or going to the park etc.

Topical signs to be learned: name, game, all, things, before, add, I, go, bring.

Crab Soccer (sports & recreation)
Equipment: one ball (soccer ball, playground ball, basketball, tennis ball), something to delineate goals (e.g., two boxes, or anything with which to mark the goals.)

Crab Soccer can be played indoors or outdoors. The aim of the game, as in regular soccer, is to propel the ball into the goal, which can be the space between two boxes laid on their sides, the space between two sneakers, or the area under a ping-pong table. But regular soccer was never played in this position! All play is accomplished in the ""crab" position! That is, players remain at all times on their hands and feet, with the face and torso turned upward. If you play outdoors, the ball can be a soccer ball, basketball, or playground ball; for indoor play, a tennis ball or rubber ball is better. You can play individually, two players can compete against each other or teams of anywhere up to a dozen or even more can play against each other. The rules are simple: Players must maintain the crab position and may only propel the ball with their feet. Any additional rules that players wish to impose, regarding fouls or off sides or out-of-bounds, are optional.

Topical signs to be learned: soccer, ball, play, team.

Create a World (fine & performing arts)

Pretend it's the beginning of the world. Ask for imaginative suggestions about how the world began. As the person describes the world's creation, have one or two others come up and become that part in the creation. Ask for more suggestions. As each succeeding item or stage of creation is suggested, have others come up to perform. (For example, air, water, the earth, clouds, wind, birds, mammals, insects, sea creatures, humans, houses, fire.) Finally, the entire group is participating in this newly created world. Afterward, a different speaker may begin creating another world.

Folklore Version

Research or read some creation tales from different peoples and incorporate them into the scene. Virginia Hamilton's *In the Beginning: Creation Stories from Around the World* (Orlando , Fla.: Harcourt Brace Jovanovich, 1988) is an excellent resource.

Topical signs to be learned: pretend, begin, world, create, perform/act, nature signs.

Create the Story Behind the Song (fine & performing arts)

Bring in several different songbook collections: folk songs, children's, popular, show tunes, and so on. Or, ask each person to copy the lyrics of two songs on separate pieces of paper and bring them in for this activity. Collect the song lyric sheets from each person. Have one person randomly choose a song lyric from the papers. Allow the person a few moments to silently read the song lyrics. To begin, the person reads the song lyrics, seated or standing, out loud to the group. Then the person tells the group about the real story behind the song lyrics. For example, why did the boy row the boat down the stream? Was he frightened? Running away? Or a foolish adventure? For the shy or reluctant participant, have him or her sit, read the lyrics out loud (or, have someone else read the lyrics out loud), and then interview the person to help him or her create a story. Be gentle and encouraging in the questioning. Use the five W's and H journalism approach: Who was the main character? Where did he or she live or come from? What was he or she doing? Why was he or she doing said activity? When was this taking place? How did it all happen?

Topical signs to be learned: song, real, story, read, create, tell, question signs.

Daylight Pajama Party

Materials: "Goodnight Moon" by Margaret Wise Brown, pajamas, blanket or sleeping bag, pillow, stuffed animal, bedtime snack (example: cookies and milk), optional props like those things found in the little bunny's room such as a bedside lamp, dollhouse, mouse etc.

Sports, Recreation, & Arts

Read the book "Goodnight Moon." Notice all the things the mother bunny in the rocking chair helps the little bunny say goodnight to in his great green room. After reading the book, set up a cozy pretend bed made of a blanket or sleeping bag and pillow. Bring a favorite stuffed toy. Keep it simple with just a few props or add many props. Wear pajamas and snuggle into the pretend bed. Have a bedtime snack. Say goodnight to everything in the room, just like the bunny in the story. Then pretend to go to sleep. Maybe take a real nap!

More Ideas: Bake sugar cookies that look like moons and stars. Play with doll furniture set up like a bedroom , with a toy baby bunny in the bed, and a mama bunny in the rocking chair. Reenact the story through play. A flannel board is also a good way to reenact the story.

Topic Signs to learn: goodnight, signs from "Goodnight Moon," toy, bed, pillow, pretend, snack, sleep, cookies, milk, play.

Doing the Pants (fine & performing arts)

The following are examples of pantomime scenes to be done individually or in pairs:
- You are a finalist in the National Bubble Gum Blowing Contest. After repeated tries, you blow the biggest bubble ever seen.
- You are a lion tamer. You enter the cage ready to perform your routine when you suddenly remember that the lions have not been fed!
- You are chasing butterflies in the woods. It's exciting until you realize you're lost and will have to spend the night in the woods.
- You're out camping. Set up camp, unload your pack, pitch a tent, chop and collect wood, rub two sticks together for a fire, fry two eggs and some bacon, eat.
- You are from France and speak very little English. You get off the boat in New York City. You ask several people where a restaurant and hotel are. People can't understand you very well.
- You're a cop in a patrol car. You see a car speeding. You chase and stop it, giving the driver a ticket.
- You are a famous actor or actress auditioning for a dog food commercial—and you hate dogs. The first dog is a dachshund, the second dog is a Saint Bernard.
- You are taken to the principle's office for fighting. At first you're angry and mouth off at the teacher. As you get to the office, you become worried. Then the principle gets you!
- You are in a haunted house. Things keep popping out at you. You are alone and very scared.
- You brag about how well you can play the violin, even though you have never played one. Then someone gives you a violin and insists that you play.
- You are a kangaroo chasing a bird and you bump into an apple tree. Apples tumble down from the tree and hit you in the head. You recover and hop away.
- You are a new window washer. You are washing outside windows twenty stories high. A strong wind starts blowing.

These scenes can be performed by the very shy and reluctant person, or by the person who can act with fine expression and detail. As long as the person performs a pant in front of the group, even for just fifteen seconds, he or she should receive encouragement and recognition.

Topical signs to be learned: act, character.

Face Pass (fine & performing arts)

This game has 2-20 players

The players are arranged in a close circle, They can be seated, if desired. The leader starts by making a funny, dramatic, or unusual face, and then the leader passes this face to the next person, who must copy the face. Both then turn to show everyone else in the group the faces made. The second person then creates a new face to pass to a third person, following the same direction. This continues around the circle until everyone has a turn. It's amazing what people will come up with, and even more so when a very serious person comes up with the most ridiculous face. If someone is having trouble coming up with a face to pass, let them know that they can say "Pass," with the option to make a face at the end if they wish. This will prevent embarrassment about participating in the game. On the other hand, you can encourage (not force) them to try, because it is great fun. Doing something quickly without thinking is probably the best way to cope.

Topical signs to be learned: leader, face, funny, show, emotion signs.

G-man (sports & recreation)

For each game use 7-10 players, you may have more than one game going at once. The leader selects a G-Man who turns their back and cover their eyes while players are lined up behind them. When the leader says, "Look," the G-Man is given one minute to look at the players, after which the G-Man turns around again and cover their eyes. The leader then motions one player to leave the line and keep out of sight. The line is then rearranged, and the G-Man turns around and is asked to name or describe the missing player. Whether the G-Man has succeeded or failed, the player who left the line becomes the G-Man for the next game.

Topical signs to be learned: line, look, minute, leave, name, describe, missing.

Hidden People (sports & recreation)

Divide into 2 or more groups (3 or 4 groups is best). Each group picks a person to hide and makes this person known to the other teams. Each team may communicate with their hidden person in any way before they leave, so that they know where they will be. At the signal, the "hidden people" hide within specified boundaries. All other players must remain in a group for five minutes. At the next signal, the search for all opposing "hidden people" begins. When found, each must return home to base without a struggle. The team of the last hidden person to be brought back is the winner.

Topical signs to be learned: person, hide, teams, other, where, search/look for, find, last, win.

Sports, Recreation, & Arts

Horse (sports & recreation)
Equipment: basketball and hoop

Choose the order in which the players will shoot at the basket. The player who shoots first is the leader; the others must copy both the type of shot he makes and place from which he shoots. If the leader fails to make his shot, he isn't penalized, but he loses his position as leader. If, however, the leader does make the shot, everyone else has one chance to try to make the shot. Any subsequent player who fails to do so acquires an H (as in HORSE, the name of the game.) Now the next round starts, with the next player in turn becoming the leader, and with the leader making a different shot from a different place. All the same rules apply, except that a player who already as an H and misses a shot now gets an O (And the next time would be an R and so on). The leader is always free to choose whatever type of shot he wants, from whatever location he wishes, including both basic shots and trick shots. A player who has all five letters of the word HORSE is out of the game. The last person left is the winner.

Topical signs to be learned: horse, basketball, ball, leader, same, different, place, out, last, win.

Human Xylophone (fine & performing arts)
Have the children line up in a group of eight. Ask the first person in line to sing a very low note. Have them memorize the sound they have just made. Then have the next person in line make a sound just slightly higher (help them with examples if necessary) and memorize it. Then the third, forth, and so on. Have them go through what they have memorized in order from the lowest to the highest. Now you have created a human xylophone and it is time to play. Have the rest of the children take turns playing the xylophone. This is done by having the human xylophone children hold their hands out. As the other children touch their hands they make their memorized sound. Each person should continue to sing the note for as long as their hand is being touched. Children can try to play familiar favorites such as *"Mary Had A Little Lamb"* on the human xylophone.

Topical signs to be learned: line up, song, music, xylophone, numbers one - eight, hear, share, band, please, thank you.

Imaginary Ball Toss (sports & recreation)
Players begin the game by tossing an imaginary ball that has no unusual characteristics. Once they have established successful reception and release patterns, new properties are assigned to the ball such as those below. The ball is now…the shape of a football, the size of a tennis ball, made of popcorn, the weight of a ping-pong ball, sticky, made of rubber, made of yarn, the shape of a basketball, the weight of a bowling ball etc.

Topical signs to be learned: ball, throw/toss, shape, size, weight, made, change, sports signs.

The Intersection (fine & performing arts, transportation)

In this activity people take a variety of points of view as ethnic and different-aged characters. It's a chance to explore how background, age, and experience can influence what one sees at an intersection.

Choose Participants: two car drivers (use chairs for cars), an old man in a 1985 Dodge truck, a well-dressed woman in her thirties driving a new BMW, a black woman with a baby standing on the corner, a young Native American boy, an elderly Japanese man, a middle-aged policeman.

The two cars collide at an intersection. Both drivers get out and start arguing. The arguing can be done at first in mime and/or with improvised dialogue. The other actors, except for the policeman, have witnessed the accident. The policeman enters, and the two drivers explain what has happened. Each of the witnesses explains what he or she saw. In giving testimony, each actor must consider his or her heritage, gender, age, and economic status, and speak with those characteristics in mind. Afterward, evaluate what each person said. What is the truth? Why might these people differ so greatly in what they claim to have witnessed? The actors might choose to play stereotyped roles, or to break those stereotypes. Then, a discussion might focus on why the character reacted in that manner. Consider what would happen if: one of the cars was a 1980 battered VW bug, an elderly person had been driving, a teenage African American had been driving.

Topical signs to be learned: different, character, car, police officer, see, explain, happen, age (old), man, lady, boy, girl, young, old.

It's the Face! (fine & performing arts, emotions)

Let's focus on the face. Repeat several phrases in a variety of different ways: fearfully, angrily, weakly, strongly, warmly, motherly, authoritatively, mysteriously, evilly, heroically. Be sure to match your tone of voice, facial expression, and body language to how you are saying and/or signing each phrase. Each time, stress a different word in the phrase: I LIKE you. I like YOU! Yeah, I like I REALLY like you.

Some phrases follow, but don't forget to make up your own.
Time for dinner!
Where is she?
Go to sleep now.
I need some money.
I don't want to.
How are you?
Come over here.
It's cold.
What's the matter?
We won.

Topical signs to be learned: emotion signs, different, say, create, face.

Sports, Recreation, & Arts

Jump Rope Rhymes (sports & recreation)

Equipment: jump rope or suitable rope (for either an individual or a group).

Johnny Over the Ocean
Johnny over the ocean , Johnny over the sea,
Johnny broke a milk bottle and blamed it on me.
I told Ma, Ma told Pa,
Johnny got a lickin', so Ha, Ha, Ha.
How many lickings did he get?
(Count until jumper misses)

Mama, Mama, I Feels Sick
Mama, Mama I feel sick:
Send for the doctor,
Quick, Quick, Quick.
How many pills will he give me?
(Count until jumper misses.)

Worms in the Jelly Bowl
Worms in the jelly bowl, Wiggle, Waggle, Wiggle
Worms in the jelly bowl, Wiggle, Waggle, Wiggle
I'm Mae West, I try to do my best
Worms in the jelly bowl, Wiggle, Waggle, Wiggle

Peal an Orange
Peal an orange, round and round (jumper turns in circle)
See if you can touch the ground; (jumper tries to touch the ground)
If you jump to twenty-two
Another turn will be given to you!
(If jumper jumps to twenty-two they are given another turn)

My Mother, Your Mother
My mother, your mother, live across the street,
Eighteen, Nineteen, Chestnut Street.
Every night they have a fight and this is what they say:
Acka backa soda cracker, Acka backa boo.
In comes (next child's name) and out goes you! (jumper runs out and new one jumps in)

Charlie Chaplin
Charlie Chaplin went to France
To teach the ladies how to dance,
First the heel and then the toe,
Around and around and around you go.

Topical signs to be learned: jump, rope, over, sea/ocean, break, milk, bottle, mother, father, tell, feel sick, send, doctor, quick, how, many, medicine, give, worm, bowl, try, do, my, best, orange, round, see, you, can, touch, ground, if, another (other), give, live, across, street, every, night, fight, what, say, in, out, come, go, teach, lady, dance, first.

Keyword (fine & performing arts, drama)

In a group, choose a who, what, and where. Each player in the group chooses a word that is related to the who, what, and where chosen. Begin improvising your scene. Whenever your word is said, if you are onstage, exit, and if you are offstage, enter (If you're not playing on a stage, leave the scene; reenter the scene when your word is said.) You must exit and enter in character. Be sure to make up a good reason to exit or enter each time your word is said. You can have a lot of fun sending your scene partners in and out by working their word into the scene, but don't forget, they can do the same to you. Continue with the game until your scene comes to an end.

Topical signs to be learned: word, who, what, where, said, leave, come, send, in, out, character, stay, continue, end.

Knots (sports & recreation)

This game can have 5-10 players for one small Knot, although if there are 12 or more players, you can make two groups. Up to 50 can play Giant Knot. A circle of players starts by standing close together facing in. They put their hands in a clump on top of one another in the middle and start mingling them. Everyone can then close their eyes and, when told, find two hands to clasp. Upon opening their eyes, check to see that all players have two different hands. To add challenge, see that players do not keep the hand of a person next to them. Players, without losing contact by hand, although not necessarily with a tight grip, try to untangle into a circle. Facing in or out does not matter.

If the knot is insoluble, allow the players to pick one grip to let go and reconnect in a better way. Then the players can see if they can unwind the knot. If not, have the group choose another grip to undo and redo. The can continue in this manner until the knot is solved. This way, there is no knot that cannot be unwound. After doing this with a group, everyone will feel a lot more comfortable with one another.
With more players, make more than one circle. Or have the whole group hold hands in a circle to start, and then have them tangle by going under or over arms without letting go of the hands to form a Giant Knot. When players cannot move any more, start to unwind. This way, having started in a circle you always end in a circle. This works with as many as 50 people.

Reminds players that if they start to feel their wrists or arms getting twisted they need not maintain a hand clasp, but merely need to keep touching. Also, remind everyone that if they are being hurt, they can simply say, "stop," and everyone will stop, thereby avoiding any painful situation.

Topical signs to be learned: hands, different, circle, move, careful, hurt, stop.

Let's Play Buried Treasure (fine & performing arts)

Materials: gold, silver or other metallic spray or brush-on paints; glitter, glitter paint, glitter glue, sequins, box for treasure chest, newspaper to protect table during

Sports, Recreation, & Arts

painting, paint and brushes, paper and pens for drawing map, used wet tea bag, items for pretend treasure: beads and hobby jewels, chocolate coins wrapped in foil, large buttons, old jewelry, plastic beads on strings, play money, small figurines or statues, small rocks, or small wood scraps.

Prepare the treasure. Some suggestions are paint the rocks gold and silver, cover the wood scraps with glitter, paint the small statues gold, or cover large buttons with glitter paint. Dry the painted items. Spread out the other items and decide what will be in the treasure chest that will be buried. Select a wooden or cardboard box for the treasure chest. The treasures can be hidden or buried in the chest, or the chest can be used to collect them after each one is found. Decorate the chest with markers and paint in any design. Find a place to bury the treasures like a sandbox, soft dirt in the garden, or behind a couch. Draw a treasure map that leads the seekers to the buried treasure. Wipe the map with a wet, used tea bag to make it look like old parchment. Find the treasure! Bury the treasure again in a new place and start all over again.

You can pretend to be pirates. Dress like pirates (eye patch, skull cap, rolled-up pants, scars, earrings), talk like pirates (Away me hearties! Ahoy there! Surrender ye swabs! Scupper that ship! Land ho!) and sing like pirates (Yo ho, yo ho, the pirate's life for me...). Or you can design flags, make sea biscuits, and write with invisible ink.

Topical signs to be learned: gold, silver, paint, paper, pens, money, statue, box, hide, find, pretend.

Lip-Synch Singer (fine & performing arts)

Choose a musical that you enjoy, such as *The Lion King, Annie,* or *Beauty and the Beast*. Or pick a tape or CD that you want to pretend you're singing. Listen to the recording a few times to get a feel for the music. Figure out who will sing which parts. Split up the parts and begin to practice. Have everyone get costumes to fit their roles—wigs, masks, or makeup will add lots of fun to the show. Get ready to sing!

Topical signs to be learned: music/sing, choose, pretend, listen, feel, practice.

Literal Phrases (fine & performing arts)

Players will have to think carefully before pantomiming the literal meaning of the following expressions:
Lend an ear, catch a train, cross the bridge when you come to it, hit the road.
This also demonstrates that expressions are not always necessarily signed using the same words, the meaning of the expression is what is important.
Try figuring out what the expressions mean and signing or acting them out. Think of other expressions to act out and sign.

Topical signs to be learned: think, real, mean, important, sign, act.

Machines (sports & recreation)

Players create a machine which can be used in a new sport of their own invention. After forming the machine, they describe how it works. Sound is optional.

Topical signs to be learned: machine, new, sports signs, invent/create, how, work, sound.

Magic Land (fine & performing arts)

Say, "Today we are going to make believe we are TV actors. Let's talk about what you saw on TV this week." Have children discuss TV shows they saw, telling what happened in the story, who the characters were, etc. Select on TV show/story mentioned by the children that has a high interest level and develop the story line (or retell the story). Review the acting situation and the rules for actors and audience. Select various children to be the characters in the play. Then say, "Now we're going to act out this story." Narrate the story, stopping at various points to let the children act and speak their parts. You man want to repeat the dramatization with different actors, so that each child has a chance to play a part in the story.

Topical signs to be learned: magic, TV, actor, see, happen, story, character, audience, narrate.

Miniature Golf (sports & recreation)

Materials: kids' golf clubs or a new sponge and a yard stick, masking tape, doormat, felt-tipped marker, ball (golf or small rubber ball), oatmeal container, shoe box, cardboard, coffee can.

If you have a set of kids' golf clubs, use them. If you don't, you can make your own by attaching a stiff new sponge to the end of a yardstick with masking tape. Use a regular golf ball or a smaller rubber ball and a doormat for the tee. Make eight or ten obstacles for the course. Here are some ideas to help you get going. For a tunnel, cut out the bottom of an empty oatmeal box and place the box on its side. For a house, turn a shoe box upside down and cut out an entrance from one end of the box and an exit from the other end. Fold a piece of cardboard in half and set it up like a tent for the ball to go through. For a ramp, take a large piece of cardboard and score it in two places to divide it in thirds. To score, run one point of a pair of scissors along the cardboard. Ask an adult assistant to help you. Bend the cardboard slightly at the score marks and place the center portion on a book. Angle the two ends to form slopping ramps. Place two or three Frisbees on the floor to form a curved fairway for the ball to go through, for a straight fairway, make two parallel rows of building blocks. Use a hula hoop to make a sand trap that you wan to avoid. Put a chair or stool in the center of the room for the ball to go under. Use an empty, clean coffee can placed on its side as the end cup. Set up obstacles around the room and use masking tape to secure them to the floor. Write numbers on the masking tape to indicate hole numbers for the course. Start at the beginning and see how many strokes it takes to get your ball through the course and into the coffee can at the end. Don't forget you're indoors, so use more finesse than force when you tee up.

Sports, Recreation, & Arts

Topical signs to be learned: golf, ball, bridge/ramp, tape, scissors, write, numbers, careful, how many.

Mirroring (fine & performing arts)

This provides a chance to work on observation and control.
In pairs, stand facing each other as if you were seeing your reflection in a mirror. First, one person of the pair makes slow, distinct motions and facial movements, and the partner mirrors these movements as accurately as possible and at the same pace. Remember, the mirror image uses the opposite part of the body. So, if the first person moves the right hand, then the mirror image moves the left. Then let the other person initiate the movements.

For a variation, select a sport and perform actions appropriate for dressing to participate in that sport. Sports such as baseball, football, track, swimming, tennis and ice skating are good to try.

Topical signs to be learned: slow, movement, face, same, choose, sport, action, clothing signs, sport signs.

Music Images (fine & performing arts)

Materials: cassette tape or cd, cassette or cd player.

Play an audiocassette/CD of different instrumental pieces, rhythms, beats, and moods. Have the group close their eyes and see the scene created by the music. In pairs, the group shares with each other what they experience and "saw" listening to the music. After this, they might volunteer to share their visions with the group. Each pair might merge their visions into an improvised dance piece or series of movement.

Topical signs to be learned: music, listen, see, share, dance, move.

News Reporter (fine & performing arts)

Materials: poster board, markers, tissue paper, tape, toilet-paper rolls.

To make microphones use a toilet-paper roll or paper-towel tube for the handle. Crumple up tissue paper (or newspaper) and tape it to one end for the microphone. Set up a desk that you and a friend can sit behind. The people who read the news are called anchors because they hold everything in place. Here are some of the parts other friends can play:
Newscaster: Who, what, where, when, why? What's going on—in the world, in your city, at your house? You can talk to the audience or interview someone else "on the scene."
Entertainment reporter: Are there any plays in your community that someone can review? Read any good books lately that can be reported on? How about a review of recent movie releases, videos worth renting, or new television shows?
Sportscaster: Talk about last weekend's Little League game or sports activities that are going on at school. Talk about your favorite professional teams.

Weather reporter: Give a summary of the day's weather and what you should be wearing if you are going outdoors.
Special interests reporter: Report on what's happening that's new or exciting—a bake sale, a school play, a car wash, someone's birthday party, new neighbors. If someone got a new pet, ask her or him to appear on the show.
Everyone should take a turn making up commercials. First try to be as serious as possible, then make your next one silly. Bet you can't keep a straight face!

Topical signs to be learned: report, reporter, special, information, desk, audience, community, city, world, movie, book, sports signs, weather signs, happen, new.

Opera Scene (fine & performing arts)
Have three to five people create their own scene or reenact a television show or commercial. The narrator and all actors sing their parts in operatic style.

Topical signs to be learned: narrator, actor, sing.

Pantomime Plugs (fine & performing arts)
Materials: pictures of electric appliances, large paper bag

Put the pictures of electrical appliances in a large paper bag. Each child selects a picture from the paper bag and pantomimes it for others to guess what it is. For example, for a clothes dryer, a child could pantomime taking clothes out of a washing machine and putting them in a dryer, watching them spin around and around until they're dry. For a stereo, a child could pretend to put on a CD and sing and dance. Other good appliances for this activity are hair dryers, vacuums, toasters, typewriters, radios, and televisions.

Topical signs to be learned: machine, picture, pick/choose, pretend, act.

Pantomime Sentences (fine & performing arts)
Clear characterizations and actions should be goals when pantomiming these sentences. You can also create your own sentences to pantomime.
You are...
a loaf of bread rising in a pan
a maid making a bed
a teenager walking your dog
a Scout helping an older person across the street
a police officer directing traffic
a clown trying to make a little child laugh
a stylist giving a haircut
a balloon blowing up and then deflating
a lion stalking your prey
a fire slowing dying out

Topical signs to be learned: character, act, sentence.

Sports, Recreation, & Arts

Parachute Games (sports & recreation)
Materials: parachute (large blanket or sheet works well), foam balls,

Merry-Go-Round
The children circle the parachute. Grab hold with their right hand and begin to go round. Then turn around and its off in the other direction.

Odd Man Out
Have the children sit around the parachute. Have them count off in numbers from 1-4. Have them lift the parachute as high as they can and as their numbers are called they get to enter the parachute. They want to go and fill in another of their numbers slots around the parachute before the trap closes.

Popcorn
Place all different size foam balls on the parachute. Have the children grab the ends and shake the chute. Watch as the popcorn pops. Have the children retrieve any balls that go astray.

Parachute Ball
Use just one ball as the children try to get the ball to go as high as they can. Then you can add another ball or 2.

The Dome
Have the children lift the parachute as high as they can. Then get inside and seal the dome by sitting on the edge.

Topical signs to be learned: parachute, circle, sit, count, shake, popcorn, ball.

Pass it Along (fine & performing arts)
Like a game of charades, this game is played in teams. It is the most fun when at least six people play, with at least three players on each team.
Each team lines up, with players either sitting or standing. The team that goes first decides what they will pass along. Will it be a piano? A feather? A crying baby? A hot slice of pizza? The funnier the made-up passed-along object, the more fun the game. The first player on the team pretends to pick up the object using exaggerated motions, and passes it to the next player, who passes it to the next player. The other team tries to guess what the object is. If the second team can't figure it out after three or four guesses, the first team reveals the object. Then the second team thinks of an object and passes it along while the first team tries to guess what it is.

Topical signs to be learned: game, team, pretend, pass, guess, and wrong.

Personal Letters (fine & performing arts)
Choose two actors to come on stage. One actor is downstage left; the other is mid-stage right. Each actor "writes" a letter to the other, including good descriptive detail in it. The first actor reads his or her letter out loud; then the second actor

answers that letter, adding his or her own personal news, insights, and feelings. Here are some possible combinations: A father in prison writes to his son, A son in a war (pick any war) writes to his mother, a sister writes to her brother on Mars, a father who deserted his daughter years ago writes to her, a college student writes to a friend who works in a fast-food restaurant, a patient writes to her psychiatrist, a person who has had a car accident writes to his insurance agent, a fan writes to a famous author (or actor or musician). Consider changing the people above, but using the same situation. For example, a mother may have deserted her daughter.

Topical signs to be learned: letter, actor, write, describe, read, answer, emotion signs.

Relays (sports & recreation)
"B" Team Relay

Divide your group up into 2 teams. Mark off a starting and turn around point. Assign a different injury to each of the different pairs of racers as follows:
      Bad knee - hop on one leg
      Hurt heel - tip toe
      Injured ankle - must keep a hand on ankle while racing
          Etc.

Chariot Relay

Two players hold their inside hands together. The third player stands behind the two and grabs hold of their outside hands. This forms one chariot. Divide the group into two or more teams and have a chariot race/relay.

Fingerspell Name Relay

Divide your group up into 2 teams. Mark off a starting and turn around point. They have to get to the turn around point and fingerspell their names. Then run back and tag the next person to go.

Flag Relay

Each team of 4-8 players should have a flag of a different color. Half of the team stands directly opposite the other half, which is 30 feet distant. The runners stand in file formation, one direction behind the other. There should be a space of 4-5 feet between each file. The first runner for each team is given a flag, one flag to a team. All players start from one side. On the word "Go!" the players with the flags race to the players opposite and hand the flag to the first runner in the line. This second runner must not step forward to take the flag. When a player hands over the flag he should go immediately to the end of the line to avoid interfering with the next player. The second runner races to the next player, etc, until every runner has carried their team's flag. The running distance may vary, depending on the age of the runners and the size of the available playing area.

Sports, Recreation, & Arts

Iceberg Relay

Equipment: construction paper "icebergs" and scissors

Divide the group into two separate groups. The students must use the icebergs to get across the raging sea to a turning point and back to their group. The first players have a set of two icebergs. By placing the first iceberg on the ground, the player can step on it and place the second iceberg further on toward the turning point. Each player must step only on the icebergs as they tries to get from the starting line and back again. The activity continues until all the students have had a chance to participate.

Movement-Challenge Relay

Equipment: one set of flash cards with the numbers 1 through 5 each on a different card.

This is a simple relay event. After dividing your class into relay teams, explain to them that they will be using different loco motor movement for this relay. The leader stands in front of the group and shows one of the flash cards. Each of the numbers will represent a different way to move from the starting line to the turning point and back.
1. Means to skip
2. Means to walk backwards
3. Means to hop on one foot
4. Means to run
5. Means to jump with two feet

Or create your own movements for each number. To make it trickier use a different number for each relay leg.

Over/Under Relay

Equipment: one ball per team

Divide your class into two or more teams. Have each team line up in a single file with the students' legs apart. On a signal, the first player takes the ball and lifts it up and over his head with his two hands. The player behind him takes the ball and brings it under his legs. The next player grabs the ball and lifts the ball up and over his head. The ball continues to go over and under all the players until it reaches the last player. The last player then runs with the ball to the front of the line and passes the ball over their head to the next player. When the original leader gets to the front of the group again, the team quickly sits down.

Partner-Pair Relay

In this relay have your students hold hands in pairs. Certain loco motor movements have to be performed. First, have the pairs run to a certain point. Skipping, hopping, leaping movements can also be used in this relay. Divide your class into smaller groups and have a partner pair relay race.

Picket Fence Relay

Equipment: one traffic cone per group

Divide your class into two groups. Each team lines up. The first player runs around the marker and places his arm to the wall. The next player runs as soon as the leader touches the wall. They go under the arm of the first player and hold up their hand. That will signal the next player to run. This continues until every player has had a turn to run.

Potato Relay

Divide players into teams. The first player is given a large tablespoon and a potato. He must carry the potato in the spoon to a goal line 10-15 feet distant and back, then hand the spoon with the potato in it to the second player who repeats the action. If a potato is dropped, the team must start over from the beginning. The first team to finish wins.

Sack-Race Relay

Equipment: one burlap sack per team

Divide the class into two or more teams. Each team lines up in a single file behind a starting line. The first player is given the sack and steps into it. On a signal, the first player has to hop to the turning point and back to their team. They then give the sack to the next player. The game continues with each player stepping into the sack and hopping around the turning point and back.

Three-Legged Relay

Equipment: one burlap bag per team

Divide your class into two teams. Each team is broken down into pairs. On a signal, the first pair places their inside legs in the burlap sack. They then have to walk around a designated turning point and back to their team. They walk by holding the back with their inside hands and stepping together first with their inside feet and then with their outside feet.

Tunnel Relay

Equipment: 20 foot strip of plastic or durable material (may be purchased in large rolls at building supply stores, hardware stores, or garden centers)

Staple or sew the sides of the plastic together to make a tunnel about three feet in diameter.
Select two teams. Each team puts half of its members at either end of the tube. Two opponents start crawling through the tunnel from opposite ends and must inevitably pass each other in the middle. When passing, they should not interfere with each other. When they reach the other end, they tag a teammate who starts back through. The first team finished wins but the most fun is watching the wiggling tunnel from the outside.

Sports, Recreation, & Arts

Tunnel-Ball Relay
Equipment: one ball per team

Have each team line up with their legs spread apart in the straddle position. The first player passes the ball under their legs to the last player in the line. The last player gets the ball and runs to the front of the group. They then straddle their legs and roll the ball under all the legs of the group to the last player. When the first player to roll the ball is in the front of the group again, all the team members sit down.

Zig-Zag Relay
Equipment: twelve traffic cones (or other similar objects)

In this relay the players have to run through a zigzag maze to a turning line and back again. Arrange the cones so that each team has its own zigzag course in front of it. On a signal, the first player runs the course and tags the hand of the next player. The first team to finish has to wait for the rest of the class to run the course.

Topical signs to be learned: pass, flag, potato, spoon, through, under, over, ball, run, line, line-up, stand, sit, jump, fingerspell, hurt, take, give, group, team, divide, return, numbers, show, way, move, touch, sack/bag.

The Queen's Headache (sports & recreation)
One student is selected to be queen. She sits in the middle of the room on a chair. The rest of the group is lined up on one side of the room. The object of the game is to quietly get from one side of the room to the other without having the Queen moan. The Queen has such a bad headache that any sound makes her moan. One by one, the students walk across the room. If the Queen hears the student and moans, that student must sit down at the spot where he was when the Queen moaned. The Queen should have her face covered so as to not be accused by the players of showing royal favoritism. After all the students have had a turn, choose another King or Queen to start the game again. This is a game that can be used from time to time whenever you need that added reassurance that your group can be quiet.
Give one of the following suggestions to the students in your group who find it easy to be quiet walkers. Walk with a book balanced on their head, walk with their shoes tied together, or walk holding one foot with the opposite hand.

Topical signs to be learned: queen, king, headache, chair, quiet, walk, sit, line, room, sound, face, cover, book, on, head, shoes.

Sequence Game (fine & performing arts)
This activity illustrates how pantomime can be used to reinforce sequencing skills. Before playing, the leader will need to create a series of cards, each having a cue and an activity to be pantomimed. (The first card is the exception as it lists only an activity.) Cards should be distributed randomly to the players, who perform the actions on their cards at their turn. They must watch carefully and correctly identify

their cue if the sequence is to be maintained. The player knows when to come to the center of the room by recognizing his or her cue as the action performed by another person. When pantomiming what is on their cards, players should face the rest of the group so that everyone can see clearly. Cues should not be numbered, as this would allow players to count cues rather than watch for clear and detailed actions. It is a good idea, however, to have a master cue sheet for the leader which notes the order of the cards. That way, if the sequence is disrupted, a quick check can reveal what happened. The leader should also keep in mind that play is made easier if the cue, written in one font or color, is at the top of the card and the action, in another font or color, is at the bottom. Wording of the action on one card and the cue on the following card should be the same.

If the sequence is not followed, as is the case when a player incorrectly identifies a cue and goes out of turn, the value of the activity is not lost. Leaders can use a sequencing game to discuss the difference between story events and plots. They should emphasize that plot is the dramatic events and the order in which they occur. Changes in the order of occurrence of events in a story alter the story. A mixed up order can illustrate to players how the same events, in changed arrangement, may transform coherence or meaning.

Instructionally, sequencing games can be adapted to many content areas. They can be written for specific topics. Or, a story known to the players or that they are reading can be divided into major episodes, each episode put on a card, and told through action. Not only do players have to read their cards silently to know the cue to watch for and the action to perform, they must also "read" the nonverbal behaviors of fellow players during pantomime. After all cards have been played, students may read them aloud, in the correct sequence, reinforcing oral reading. The application of the activity to language arts is obvious. Another application is to develop sequencing games which are more recreational. If particular holidays or special events are celebrated, sequence games can enhance the festivities.

Topical signs to be learned: leader, activity/do, watch/look, wrong, event, topic, story.

Show Producer (fine & performing arts)

Materials: old clothes, old shoes, old hats, makeup, props.

Write a script or outline for your show. Give parts to all the players. Design and make costumes and props. Practice the show until it's the way you want it. Invite an audience. Perform your show. Take a bow!

Topical signs to be learned: clothing signs, write, practice, audience, bow.

Silly Antics (fine & performing arts)

Materials: index cards, markers.

Make the Silly Cards by thinking up silly antics to write on each index card. A simple, clear drawing may be used instead of words, if desired. Some ideas are: sing Mary Had a Little Lamb, you are a tiny seed growing, hop up and down on one foot, dig a hole and jump in, climb up Jack's beanstalk, pretend you are asleep, kiss your

Sports, Recreation, & Arts

mother goodnight, blink your eyes, stick out your tongue, go swimming, clap your hands and jump up and down, swim in Jell-O, cry like a little baby; row, row, row your boat; go fishing and catch a whale, smile with your lips glued shut, plant a flower, sign/sing a song by yourself, spin around 3 times, but don't fall; take your fish for a walk.

Place the cards in a pile on the floor. To play the game: Sit beside the Silly Cards. The first player draws a card and must perform whatever the card says. Now it's the next person's turn, and so on. Or players can select specific cards for other players to act out. Everyone performs the embarrassing, silly antics described on the cards. Laughing is required!

Topical signs to be learned: silly, write, draw, act/perform, play, game, laugh.

Slide Show (fine & performing arts, drama)
Here's a way to make a vacation slide show very interesting.
One person is the presenter; everyone else is part of the slide show. The presenter begins telling the story of her vacation. Throughout the story, the presenter says, "next slide please." The other players strike a pose just like people in a photo from a vacation. The presenter uses this group pose to tell a story. The players keep their pose, as if they are an actual slide, until the presenter says, "next slide, please." Then the players change their pose, and the presenter continues the story of her vacation, explaining this new pose as if it where the very next slide from her vacation. The presenter can set up how the players will pose by saying something like, "in my next slide you will see us climbing the mountain. Next slide please," and the players pose as if they are climbing a mountain. Or the presenter can let the players create a picture on their own by giving the next slide no introduction. In this case, the presenter must somehow work this new pose into the story. Continue the scene until the presenter has finished the story of her vacation.

Topical signs to be learned: tell, story, next, photo, use, change, explain, finished.

Some Twists of the Tongue (fine & performing arts)
Not only are tongue twisters fun to say and good for loosening up the group, but they also emphasize concentration and articulation. Good practice! Try repeating these several times in a row.
Many marbles made Marvin merry.
Three gray gees in the green growing grass.
The sixth sheik's sixth sheep's sick.
Lavinia Lyman lost leaking lemon liniment.
I never felt feel flat like that felt flat.
An old scold sold a cold coal shovel.
Percy Pig is plump and pink! I like plump pink pig—I think.
White Whitney whistled while he whitewashed the fence.
Six long, slim, slick, slimy, slender saplings swaying in the springtime sunshine.
How much wood could a woodchuck chuck, if a woodchuck could chuck wood? A woodchuck would chuck all the wood he could if a woodchuck could chuck wood.

Topical signs to be learned: say, practice, several/few, time, fun.

Sports Sound Journal (sports & recreation)

Materials: recording of sports sounds, paper; markers, crayons, or pencils.

Players should listen to the following sounds. In this sound journal they describe and draw the following sport sounds: a bat hitting a baseball, a foot kicking a football, an iron striking a golf ball, a basketball hitting the hoop board, a tennis ball hitting the racquet, a beach ball hitting the sand.

Topical signs to be learned: listen/sound, describe, draw, sport signs.

Spinning Feelings (fine & performing arts, emotions)

Materials: plastic coffee can lid, heavy paper plate, square of cardboard, brass bracket, pencil, scissors, permanent markers, index cards.

To construct the spinner: Cut an arrow from the plastic coffee can lid. Punch a hole in it with the points of a pair of scissors and set aside. Trace the paper plate with a pencil on a square of cardboard. Cut the cardboard 1" to 2" larger than the traced circle. Poke a hole through the center of the paper plate with a pencil point or scissors tips, and another hole through the center of the cardboard square. Join the plate and the square with a brad/brass bracket. To do this, push the brad/brass bracket through the plastic arrow, through the plate, through the cardboard, and open it to the back of the cardboard. Now spin the plate. If it does not spin, make the hole in the plate larger or loosen the brad/bracket a little.

To make the feelings circle: Draw two lines crossing each other directly through the center of the plate to divide it into four equal pie shapes. First draw light pencil lines, and when happy with the lines, go over them with a permanent marker. In the first pie shape space, draw a happy face. In the next space, draw a sad face. Draw a surprised face and an angry face in the last two spaces. Other feelings faces could be drawn instead of any of these four, such as: sleepy, bored, goofy, giddy, dreamy, thrilled, melancholy.

To make the situation cards: Write situations, such as any similar to the following: a goat is eating your shoe, a space ship landed in your backyard, it's lunch time, nothing to eat but candy bars for breakfast, lunch, and dinner!; telephone call for you, two monsters are at your door.
To play: Pick a situation card and then spin the spinner to see which emotion you must portray when acting out that situation.

Topical signs to be learned: plate, paper, scissors, pencil, write, draw, face, emotion signs, act.

Spud (sports & recreation)

The game begins when one of the children throws the ball into the air, then calls the name of one of the children. That child has to stop running away, come back and get the ball. When they do they yell "spud". Everyone must then stop where they are.

Sports, Recreation, & Arts

The person then throws the ball at one of the frozen players. If she hits the person then they are it and have to throw the ball into the air and calls a name. If she misses then she is it. And so it goes for approximately 15 minutes.

Topical signs to be learned: ball, throw, name, stop, run, come, get.

Stand-up Comedian (fine & performing arts)

The best "bits" (ideas) for your comedy routine usually come from things that have happened in your everyday life. Use examples from family gatherings like holidays, family reunions, or birthday parties. Another good source of ideas is from adventures like going to the zoo or circus, traveling on vacation, or funny things that happened at school. When you think of funny things that have happened in the past, write down little stories about them. You can read them aloud for your audience or ad-lib from them as part of your comedy routine. You should make sure you have at least two jokes or funny parts every minute. The important thing is not to make fun of other people. (That's not funny!) But you can be funny making jokes about yourself. Wear something bright and colorful that shows you are there to have fun. Add other funny costume pieces like funny glasses or a crazy wig—anything to get people in the mood to laugh!

Topical signs to be learned: happen, holiday signs, family signs, funny, write, story, read, audience, joke (tease), and laugh.

Steal the Bacon (sports & recreation)

Divide players evenly into two teams. Line them up in two rows facing each other about 20 feet apart, the bacon in the middle. Each person in line receives a number from one to whatever the number of players on the team. The ones of each team or on opposite sides of the lines (The last player from one team, say number twelve, would be facing the person who is number one on the opposite team). Any object can be the bacon such as a block of wood or rolled up newspaper. The leader calls numbers and decides points in disputes.

When the game starts, the leader calls a number, e.g. "two," where upon #2 from each side makes a run for the bacon. The person who secures the bacon makes a point for their side. The game should continue at least until each person has had a chance to steal the bacon or until one team has reached a determined amount of points.

Topical signs to be learned: team, line, bacon, number signs, run.

Story Starters (fine & performing arts)

Brainstorm some characters and settings with the group. Here are some possibilities for characters: a lizard, an orphan girl, a spoiled rich lady, an old hermit, a mad inventor, a tusk less walrus, a business woman, a house father. Here are some settings possibilities: a jungle, the moon, prehistoric cave, computer store, under a house, a pirate ship, a zoo, under the ocean.

Have the group make up different combinations of the characters and settings. How about a story about a tusk less walrus who lives on a pirate ship, or a mad inventor who owns a computer store, or an old hermit who finds a home in a cage in the zoo, or an orphan boy who lives in the jungle and becomes a house father? Brainstorm the plot or theme of the story. It can be jealousy, finding a friend, solving a mystery, searching for treasure, meeting a monster in the jungle. Anything! With these three categories, there's a wealth of story possibilities to tell or write. For more fun, write each group on pieces of paper and place them each in separate bags and choose one from each (Characters, setting, plot/theme). See what odd combinations you'll end up with!

Topical signs to be learned: character, setting (place), theme (topic), tell, write, story, paper, choose.

Tag Games (sports & recreation)

Equipment: nerf ball, bean bag or other soft ball or object; colored paper squares, four basketballs, flashlight

Ball Tag

Use a nerf ball (soft foam), bean bag, or other soft ball or object. "It" has the ball which he throws (gently) at any other player. The other player may attempt to dodge. If they are hit, they become "it."

Chain Tag

The players are scattered around a designated area with boundaries. Two captains are chosen. At the starting signal, the two captains try to tag as many players as possible. The first person tagged links hands with the captain, and they run together, As each person is tagged, he joins the line. The line may encircle a player, but only the captain may tag him. The longest line wins and the last player to escape being tagged wins. If the lines are fairly even, they may be used to form lines for another game.

Chinese Tag

The tagged player is "it" and must hold the part of the body where he was tagged.

Color Tag

This game is played the same as plain tag but there are colored square scattered around—colored paper will do. Players are safe when standing on a colored square but a player may stand on each color only once. For example, if he takes refuge from "it" on a red square, he must not use a red square again, but must next run to another color.

Cross Tag

"It" chases another. Some other player may run in between "it" and the one being chased. This crossing goes on indefinitely and "It" must always chase the last person who ran between him and the one he was chasing. Anyone who is tagged becomes "it."

Sports, Recreation, & Arts

Dribble Tag (sports & recreation)

This game is played on a basketball court. Select four players to be It. These four players will have the basketballs. It is up to them to dribble the ball and try to tag as many players as possible. The players who are tagged must sit down. While it may not seem fair that the taggers must dribble the basketball, the four players can easily "track down" certain players by cooperating together. You can also play another variation of this game by having eight players be IT. These eight players can then dribble and pass the basketball in attempts to tag the other player. Once again, the taggers must be dribbling the ball when tagging the other students. Once all the students have been tagged, start the game over by selecting new players to be IT.

Flashlight Tag

This game must be played in deep shade or darkness. "It" has only to zap a wanderer in the dark with a beam of light from a flashlight to tag them and thus convert the wanderer to "it." Those being chased must keep on the move to avoid being zapped. It's best to set boundaries and provide adult supervision to keep younger children from getting lost or scared. Check the terrain out in daylight to make sure there are no holes, water or other dangers.

Hug Tag

Game can have 10-50+ players. The game is played by choosing an It. The It carries a ball or other object so that everyone knows who It is. It tries to catch and touch another player, making them It. When the It tags someone, the ball or object is passed on to the new It. Other players who are not It can avoid being tagged by either running away or hugging another player. Hugs can last for only three seconds, however, and the It can count to three to make sure.

To make the game more interesting, more than one person can be It at the same time, thereby increasing the action. After a while, another challenge is to require more than two people in a hug—try three, four, or more? Last, for the truly daring, players can be tagged in a hug if the It can touch the abdomen of any person in a hug. The result is closer hugs. This last measure is not for all groups, but if players are open to the idea, it can add a lot of fun. Any way you play this game, people seem to get closer.

Remind players to look out for other players. Modifications can be made for players who are a bit shy or reluctant to hug, such as putting hands on one another's shoulders, holding hands, or maybe even touching elbows. In extreme circumstances where players do not want to touch at all, having them hold on to a piece of clothing (like a sleeve) of another player might work.

Link Tag

Designate a base. Two players link hands and try to tag the other players. These two players are the only ones who can tag others throughout the game. All those tagged take their places between the first two players, all linking hands. The chain grows longer with each new addition. The players being chased may try to break the chain by forcing clasped hands apart while avoiding the two players at either end of the chain. If the chain is broken, it must be joined again before the tagging can continue. Players dropping out to rest must return to base and remain there until they re-enter the game. Players may not return to base to escape being tagged.

Shadow Tag

Requires a sunny day. To tag a person, "it" must step on that person's shadow.

Swat Tag

"It" tags others with a swatter (rolled up newspaper etc.) then drops it. The new "it" must pick up the swatter and continue. Remind the students to be gentle when swatting each other.

Topical signs to be learned: catch, touch, ball, cooperate, line, hug, color signs, join, runaway.

Talking Ball (fine & performing arts)

Materials: ball

Sit in a circle (or across from each other if there are two people playing). One person holds the ball and, while they hold the ball, they are the storyteller. The storyteller begins telling a story about anything. After a few sentences, the storyteller tosses the ball to someone else. Now they are the new storyteller. The new storyteller continues the story where the old storyteller left off. The second person must build off the story that was started by the first person. After a few sentences, the ball is passed again and the story continues with a new storyteller. Keep tossing the ball until the story comes to an end. You can only talk if you are holding the talking ball. You can toss the ball at the end of a sentence or in the middle. If the ball toss is in the middle, the new storyteller continues the story exactly from where the first person stopped. Listen closely to the story, so when it's your turn to be the storyteller, everything makes sense.

Topical signs to be learned: ball, sit in circle, pass (give), story, tell, storyteller (narrator), sentence, few, end, listen, throw.

Think Quickly! (fine & performing arts)

This is an exercise that emphasizes listening to others and making responses that require quick thinking. Invite five volunteers to form a line or a semicircle. Whomever you point to must begin talking, without pauses, on any topic. When you point to a different person, that person must immediately pick up the topic of the

Sports, Recreation, & Arts

first speaker and continue on, changing the topic when he or she can. Then point to the third person, and so on. If one of the five becomes confused, pauses more than five seconds, or doesn't continue the topic, then that person must sit down. Get another volunteer to take their place and continue on.

Topical signs to be learned: listen, respond, think, quick, volunteer, topic, change, confused, continue, sit.

Those –*ly* Ending Words (fine & performing arts)

Materials: paper and pen or pencil.

Choose three people: two to be actors and one to be recorder-director
The two actors leave the room. The recorder-director then asks the rest of the group for suggestions of –*ly* ending words : lovingly, hatefully, spitefully, proudly, ferociously, vacantly, bossily, cowardly etc. The recorder-director writes down several of the suggested words. The two actors return to the room. The recorder director chooses any of the words at random and calls out the –*ly* ending word. The actors must immediately improvise a situation based on the word as the main emotion. The recorder-director calls out "Freeze!" and gives the next word. The actors switch to a different situation that demonstrates the second –*ly* word.

Topical signs to be learned: actor, act, leave, write, word, emotion signs, freeze (stop), next.

Through the Door (fine & performing arts)

Choose on player to be the director. Everyone else makes a line backstage (or out the door or behind the screen). The director should not be able to see the players and should not know their order in line. The director calls out a character. It can be a famous person or a type of worker. For example, the director may call out, "cheerleader." The first player in line comes out and walks across the stage (or room) as a cheerleader. She may speak if she wants to, but the most important thing is to walk like a cheerleader. After she has walked across the stage or room, she goes back through the door and to the end of the line. The director then calls out another character, such as "Captain Hook," and the next actor in line comes out as Captain Hook, walks across the stage/room, then gets back in line. The game continues until everyone has played a number of characters. This game can get humorous because the players don't know what character they will be asked to play, and the director doesn't know who is next in line. The director may call out, "Snow White," and a boy may be next, or the director may call out "a mouse" and the tallest person in the group may be next. The player must give his or her best performance, no matter how different the part may be. For ideas of characters, think of your favorite stories, famous people, or different types of work people perform. Or you can play Reverse Through the Door where the players decide what character they are performing and the director has to guess who he or she is.

Topical signs to be learned: character, act, like, through, door, walk, line (line-up).

Tin Can Bowling (sports & recreation)

Equipment: softball, 10 tin cans, backdrop (for behind pins).

You will need a level stretch of ground for this activity. Set up the "pins" with a backdrop behind them. Experiment with the terrain to judge how long the alley should be. It will also depend on the age of the bowlers. Have someone who sets up the pins.

Topical signs to be learned: ball, ground, long, should, age.

Treasure Hunt (sports & recreation)

This can be planned for a specific theme. For example a pirate hunt, a storybook with each person a different character, a nature hunt, and Indian hunt using Indian signs for clues. Use clues everyone will understand. Lay the trail backwards—decide where the treasure will be hidden, hide it, then write clues. Don't hide the treasure too near the starting place. Put the hardest clue in the middle of the hunt, allowing stragglers to catch up. Read the first clue to everyone out loud to get everyone off to the same start.

Topical signs to be learned: hunt (search), character, nature, Indian, sign, understand, trail, hide, find.

Tuck Jump (sports & recreation)

This stunt is performed by having the player try to jump high enough to assume a tuck position while in the air. The tuck position should be performed quickly, with the student bringing their knees into their chest and wrapping their arms about their knees. This movement should be rapid enough to allow the performer to land on the ground in a standing position.

Topical signs to be learned: jump, knee, fast, ground, stand.

Tug-of-War (sports & recreation)

Equipment: rope.

Several volunteers can serve as broadcasters who provide the "play-by-play" in response to team actions for a tug-of-war that is being shown on television. Other players form the competing teams.

Topical signs to be learned: team, volunteer, action.

Ball Player's Game

Equipment: balls, drum, music.

Using a variety of balls, players may bounce them to the beat of a drum, to chants or poems, or to recorded music. It is suggested to approach practice with larger balls (e.g. volleyball size) at a moderate temp. Older players with well-developed skills may be invited to select smaller balls and use faster tempos.

Sports, Recreation, & Arts

Topical signs to be learned: ball, bounce, drum, music, slow, fast.

Un-volleyball (sports & recreation)
Materials: volley ball and net.

This game is played like regular volleyball with one exception. If the person hits the ball over the net then they have to cross over and join the opposing team.

Topical signs to be learned: volleyball, join, other, team.

Walk Through Time (fine & performing arts)
Have the group form a circle and begin walking. As they walk, call out characters: toddler, drunk, elderly person, cowboy, soldier, weakling, strongman, movie star, pregnant woman, and so on. Each person then assumes a walk and a manner that would be typical of that character. As a variation, call out the "character walks" in reverse.

Topical signs to be learned: circle, walk, character, age, man, woman, boy, girl, baby.

The What-Ifs (fine & performing arts)
Another story-starter approach is to simply take some time to let minds wander—even off to the Land of the Absurd of the What-ifs. So:
What if you suddenly discovered you had an identical twin?
What if you could fly by simply pressing your nose?
What if you could attach body parts to make a strange living creature?
What if you found your mother was an alien?
What if you were a rock and could think, feel, and move?
What if you could choose to go on the most exciting adventure possible?
Make up your own What –ifs to get the imaginations rolling.

Topical signs to be learned: what, if, find, twin, look, same, fly, nose, mother, think, feel, move, rock, choose, exciting, create.

Water Walking (fine & performing arts)
This may be done in pantomime first and then later with improvised sounds and exclamations. Everyone stands and walks in a circle. Imagine water flowing into the room, first covering your feet, thighs, and then your waist, neck, and finally over the top of your head—but you discover that you can breathe underwater. Adjust your body movements and gestures according to the changing depth of the water. Then each person becomes a sea creature. After a few moments more, the water recedes slowly. Change your movement in reverse with the lowering of the water.

Topical signs to be learned: walk, circle, water, cover, under, change, movement/move, sea animal.

When you know the place, Join in (pantomime)

This activity is based upon the concept that many locations are recognizable because of the endeavors which occur there or, similarly, through association of people and places. To begin, one person comes to the center of the room and pantomimes someone engaged in an activity related to a specific place. As other players recognize the locale, they join. They must, however, join as a different character engage in a different action. After each site playing is completed, the last player to join and the first player tell where they are. If the activity is done clearly, both will be in the same place.

Topical signs to be learned: know, place, activity (do), join, where.

You Came from Another Planet (fine & performing arts)

You're an alien whose mission is to visit Earth from a distant planet and then to return with your evaluation of Earthlings. It's now time to report on what you observed and to evaluate human behavior. Discuss, in the English you learned, some of the following from your alien point of view, using examples of what you experienced: How humans treat each other. What entertainment they like. Fears they have. What humans value. Humans' appearance and dress. Types of transportation. Use of language and sound. Music. Or other things involving culture and planet Earth.

Topical signs to be learned: earth, report, what, see, English, learn, how, what, afraid, look, like, transportation signs, language, sound, music, other.

Crafts

Can Drums (fine & performing arts)

Materials: Various assortment of different size cans (cleaned), packaging tape, stickers, construction paper, markers, glue, chopsticks.

Get each child to bring in 3 cans from home. Switch them around so they each can have a various assortment of sizes. Cut out construction paper large enough to cover each of the cans. Decorate with markers and stickers then glue onto the cans. Turn them upside down and place together, then use packing tape to tape them all together. Have the children tap with their fingers to produce different sounds. Now try it with chopsticks (warn them not to tap too hard or they will break). Now we are ready to play. Compare the sounds each of the different drums make. Play the drums to one of your classes favorite songs having half the class play the drums, while the other half sign. Then switch and play again.

Topical signs to be learned: Music, song, drums, paper, glue, scissors, colors, hear, share, please, thank you.

Castanets (fine & performing arts)

Materials: 1" x 6" strips of heavy cardboard, string, bottle caps, markers, packing tape, scissors.

Sports, Recreation, & Arts

Before beginning have leader use a hammer and nail to create two holes very close to one another in the middle of the bottle caps, need 2 bottle caps for every castanet to be made (per child). Decorate both sides of the strip of cardboard with marker, then fold in half and cover the outside of the folded cardboard with a strip of packaging tape, trimming the edges. Poke two holes close together ¾ of an inch from the open ends of the castanet. Secure the bottle cap with the string through the two holes in the cardboard and the bottle cap, being sure to tie it on the outside, with the serrated edges of the bottle cap touching the cardboard. Now we are ready to play. Compare the sounds each of the different castanets makes. Play the castanets to one of your classes favorite songs having half the class play the castanets, while the other half sign. Then switch and play again.

Topical signs to be learned: Music, song, string, glue, colors, hear, share, scissors, please, thank you.

Face-Paint Stencils (fine & performing arts)

Materials: tempera paint-consider using Biocolor nontoxic paint because it peels off when dry and is entirely washable, make-up sponges (slightly damp), face lotion, paper, scissors, pie pan or other plate, mirror (optional), tape, pencil, selection of brushes like cotton swab, eyeliner brush, make-up brush, small paintbrush.

Place small puddles of each color of tempera paints on the pie pan. Squirt or drop a teaspoon of face lotion into each paint color to make removal easier later. Mix the lotion and paint together with a brush or swab. Cut a small design, shape, or other stencil from the paper. A bold design like a star, flower, or cat without a lot of detail works the best. If working alone, look in the mirror for the next steps. Or friends can paint friends. Hold the stencil on the forehead or cheek. Use a little tape to hold the stencil, if desire. Press the damp makeup sponge into a selected color of paint. Dab it on the edge of the pans or on a scrap of paper to remove extra paint. Now gently dab the paint on the stencil, covering the skin that shows through the stencil. Let dry a moment. Remove the stencil and the painted design will remain. The stencil can be used again, but is most effective the first time. Do as many stencil designs as desired. Explore the use of the brushes and swabs for outlining or mixing colors on the skin. When dry, remove paints with soap and water, or gently remove with face lotion on paper towels or tissues. You can also paint designs without stencils on the face. Or paint the face to look like favorite animals, characters, or themes.

Topical signs to be learned: face, paint, draw, shape, paper, scissors, color signs.

Flip-Books (fine & performing arts)

Materials: paper, pencil, stapler.

Use 10 to 12 3 x 2 ¼" pieces of paper. One of these small papers is to be shaded with a pencil so as to make a "carbon" sheet. The others are to be neatly stacked. With a bending motion, push the stack neatly and evenly to create the smooth beveled surface. Turn the stack over and place staple on one short end of book. Position the stack with the two clamped ends of the staple uppermost. Place the carbon sheet face down under the top sheet of the flip-book and draw a cartoon with a pencil.

When the cartoon is finished, the carbon is to be removed and placed under the next lower sheet. Small changes are then made in the lightly transferred image and then the rest of the image is penciled in exactly as it appears. This process with its transferred image and minute changes in details continues until the book is complete. When you riffle the top edge of the flip-book with your thumb—your own animated cartoons spring to life! The possibilities here are endless.

Topical signs to be learned: book, paper, pencil, draw.

Flowerpot Bells (fine & performing arts)

Materials: 3 different size clay flowerpots, 3 – 1 foot lengths of heavy cord, wooden spoon, long thin board 1" (w) x 2" (h) x 18" (l) , hammer (adult use only), nails(adult use only).

Group project (4). Have the children tie a large knot on one end of the 1 foot lengths of cord. Thread the cord through the hole in the bottom of the flower pot, with the knot on the inside and long piece of cord coming through the hole with the pot sitting upside down on the table. Nail the cords evenly apart so that the bells have at least 2" of space in between each. Now we are ready to play. Compare the sounds each of the different flowerpot bell makes. Play the bells to one of your classes favorite songs having ¼ the class play the bells, while the others sign. Then switch and play three more songs until everyone gets a turn.

Topical signs to be learned: music, song, bells, hear, share, please, thank you.

Framing (fine & performing arts)

Materials: paper or cardboard larger than picture to be displayed, paste or glue, tape (preferably masking tape), pencil, steel-edged ruler, scissors, single-edged razor blade or hobby knife.

Mounting: To mount a picture is to affix it for display purposes to a larger sheet of paper or cardboard. For classroom use, a picture can be mounted using paste, glue, rubber cement, or even a stapler.

Matting: To mat a picture is to display it through a window cut in a large piece of paper or cardboard. The simplest mats are made of paper. Although you can cut a pretty fair paper mat with scissors, a sharp single-edged razor blade held against a steel-edged ruler will do the best job. Cardboard mats are by far the best but they are expensive and difficult to cut. Here a steel-edged ruler and a very sharp cutting edge are required. Do not try to cut through a cardboard mat with the first stroke of the blade. As long as the first cut is clean and accurate, you can use as many strokes as you wish. If you are cutting many mats, change blades often. Be sure you have an old piece of cardboard or a cutting board under your mat-to-be or you may also be cutting a window in your work surface. If your first attempt is less than perfect, you can often correct ragged edges with a piece of fine sandpaper. Although masking tape is preferred for attaching a picture to the back of a mat, for classroom use one could just as easily use cellophane tape or even paste or glue.

Sports, Recreation, & Arts

Cuffs: Sometimes a picture can be greatly enhanced by the use of a small inner mount or mat. This small inner board is called a cuff. A mounted cuff is easy to make for it is just another piece of paper cut slightly larger than the picture. A matted cuff is an inner mat whose window is slightly smaller than the window of the outer mat.

You can choose different colors for your mats and mounts. You can choose white or off-white for a traditional approach (sometimes a pen line drawn around the picture will help to "contain the eye.") You can use dark-against-light/light-against-dark for a dramatic result. Or choose any variety of color that compliments your picture.

Four good framing rules:
1. The border surrounding a picture is normally of equal width on three sides but slightly larger at the bottom.
2. Smaller pictures look best against relatively large borders; larger pictures look best against smaller borders.
3. If you are framing with colored paper, select the color of your mount or mat from one of the predominate tones of the pictures.
4. The color of the cuff is also chosen from one of the colors in the picture. Dark pictures often look good with a light or brightly colored cuff against a dark background; lighter pictures, a dark cuff against a light background.

Here are some convenient paper sizes for quick and easy mounting:

- for 9 x 12" pictures use a 12 x 15" construction paper mount
- for 12 x 18" pictures use an 18 x 24" construction paper mount
- for 8 ½ x 11" pictures use a 9 x 11 ½ " construction paper cuff and a 12 x 14 ½ " mount.

Jingle Bracelet (fine & performing arts)
Materials: 1 ft. lengths of ribbon, large wooden beads, jingle bells.

Have the children string the beads and 3 jingle bells onto the ribbon, being sure to have an equal amount of beads (4 or so) between each bell. Tie both ends together in a square knot so that the bells and beads stay close together. Compare the sounds of each bracelet by having the children shake them, tap them on their other hand and thigh. Have half of the children use their bracelet to compliment the class singing and signing the familiar song *"Jingle Bells"*. Then switch and sign, sing and play again.

Topical signs to be learned: music, song, band, bell, colors, hear, share, please, thank you.

Jug Shaker (fine & performing arts)
Materials: ½ gallon plastic jug (milk, juice) with handle and lid, jingle bells, medium sized plastic or wooden beads, duck or packaging tape, glue, stickers.

Have the children work in groups of 4. Have them fill their jugs from ¼ to ½ full with beads and jingle bells. Glue the lid on, adding tape for extra support. Have the children decorate the jugs as they wish with stickers. Compare the noise made by each of the jugs. Shake them along to familiar tunes as you sing them. Now we are ready to play. Compare the sounds each of the different jug shakers make. Play the shaker jugs to one of your classes favorite songs having ¼ of the class play the shaker jugs, while the others sign. Then switch and play three more songs until everyone gets a turn.

Topical signs to be learned: music, song, band, colors, hear, share, please, thank you.

Makeup Morgue (fine & performing arts)

Materials: pen, magazines, paper, scissors, glue.

Begin by labeling seven different pieces of paper with the following headings: old age, youth, glamorous, animals, hair, facial hair, and unusual characters. Look through magazines and cut out pictures of people who depict your several different categories: for old age page, find pictures of older people; for youth, find pictures of babies, kids, or young adults/teens; for glamorous, look for models and pictures of wealthy or elegantly dressed people; animals can include real or cartoons; for hair, look for pictures that show unusual hairstyles; for facial hair, find pictures of men with beards and/or mustaches; and for your unusual characters page, look for people who are out of the ordinary such as superheroes, cartoon humans, elves, space aliens, and so on. Glue the pictures onto the appropriate page. See if you can fill up an entire page for each category.

Topical signs to be learned: paper, magazines, pictures, scissors, glue, old, young/youth, animals, hair, face, characters.

Musical Kazoo (fine & performing arts)

Materials: Toilet tissue tube, 4" x 4" colorful cellophane square, rubber band, markers, stickers, scissors

Use markers and stickers to decorate the tube. Place the cellophane around one end of the tube and hold it in place with a rubber band. Have the children blow in the uncovered end to hear the sound. Then have the children add a hole or two, with scissors, to the tube and play, covering and uncovering the holes. Now we are ready to play. Compare the sounds each of the different kazoo makes. Play the kazoos to one of your classes favorite songs having half the class play the kazoos, while the other half sign. Then switch and play the song again or play another class favorite.

Topical signs to be learned: music, song, horn, band, paper, glue, scissors, colors, hear, share, please, thank you.

My Own TV

Materials: appliance cardboard box, strong and large (big enough to crawl inside); felt pen or dark crayon, sharp knife (adult use only), stickers or labels (optional), masking or duct tape.

Sports, Recreation, & Arts

Draw a TV screen on one side of the box. Draw it as large as possible. Draw additional TV parts such as knobs, buttons, speakers. Stickers or labels can also be used for this step. Cut out the hole for the screen with the knife (adult only). Fold the flaps out on bottom of the box. Tape the box flaps to the floor to help keep the box from wiggling and collapsing. Crawl into the box and pretend to be on television.

More Ideas
Make up a commercial. Hold an empty cereal box, toy, or other prop to sell. Sing a song or act out a favorite book or story. Ask a friend to change the "channel" for a new "program." Use an old cabinet-style TV set with all the parts removed.

Topical signs to be learned: TV, movie, box, pen, crayon, draw.

Paper Plate Tambourine (fine & performing arts)

Materials: Heavy duty paper plate, jingle bells, single hole, paper punch, tempura paint, paintbrushes, markers, glitter, glue, yarn.

Have the children punch 3 sets of 2 evenly spaced holes around the paper plate. Decorate with glitter, markers or paint. Use yarn to tie 3 jingle bells to the plate. Once dry we are ready to make music. Now we are ready to play. Compare the sounds each of the different tambourine makes. Play the tambourine to one of your classes favorite songs having half the class play the tambourine, while the other half sign. Then switch and play the song again or play another class favorite.

Topical signs to be learned: music, song, band, bells, paper plate, glue, scissors, colors, hear, share, please, thank you.

Pie Tin Cymbals (fine & performing arts)

Materials: Aluminum pie tins, small door knobs (or cork), screws, washer, nail, screwdriver.

Push the nail through the center of the pie tin to make a small hole. Place a screw through the washer, then through the pie tray (facing outside). Then put a knob on the bottom of the pie tin, screwing it onto the outward facing screw. Tighten with screw driver. Each child makes two. Gently hit them together. Now we are ready to play. Compare the sounds each of the different cymbals makes. Play the cymbals to one of your classes favorite songs having half the class play the cymbals, while the other half sign. Then switch and play the song again or play another class favorite.

Topical signs to be learned: music, song, band, hear, please, thank you.

Popcorn Maraca (fine & performing arts)

Materials: Plastic film canisters with lid, popsicle sticks, popcorn kernels, rice, dry beans, construction paper, glue, musical stickers, markers, tempura paint, paint brushes.

Have each child make 2 maracas. Fill the film canisters about ¼ full of with either rice, popcorn kernels or dry beans. Cut a hole in the lid to insert the popsicle stick (may be best for teacher to do ahead of time). Put a small amount of glue into the lid outer rim of the lid, then close the lid securely to the film canister. Then have the children write their names on one end of the Popsicle stick. Insert the end without the name into the canister and glue where it enters the canister. Cut out a piece of construction paper to go around and cover the film canister, glue onto the canister, and let dry for a moment. Decorate with paint, markers or stickers as children wish. Let sit long enough to insure Popsicle stick is secure than make music. Now we are ready to play. Compare the sounds each of the different maraca makes. Play the maraca to one of your classes favorite songs having half the classes play the maraca, while the other half sign. Then switch and play the song again or play another class favorite.

Topical signs to be learned: music, song, drums, paper, popcorn, rice, paint, glue, scissors, colors, hear, share, please, thank you.

Puppets

Elephant Puppet

Materials: felt, scissors, needle, thread, googly eyes, button.

Cut out two elephant shapes from pieces of felt. They must be large enough to fit onto your hand and the trunk should be just a little wider than your finger. Remember also to allow room for the seam. Now sew the two pieces together, all around the head and trunk, leaving just the opening for your hand. Cut out and stitch on ears, eyes, and tusks. The trunk can be worked with your longest finger.

Finger Puppets

Materials: paper or felt, glue or tape (or needle and thread), markers or crayons, paper scraps, other items to decorate puppets.

Roll a piece of paper around your finger so that it fits quite well without falling off every time you move it. Stick the paper together. Or roll a piece of felt around your finger that fits well without falling off every time you move it and glue it or stitch it. Decorate with markers, crayons, paper scraps, or other items.

Finger Puppet Theatre

Materials: strong paper plate, scissors, construction paper scraps, glue, sticky dot or white label (optional), permanent marker.

Cut a slit in the middle portion of the paper plate. With scraps of construction paper, cut shapes and things to create a scene on the plate with trees, clouds, or any other ideas. Glue them on the plate (Items can cover the slit, but must be cut apart to keep the slit open.) Take a permanent marker and draw a face on the pointer finger. A plain sticky dot or a white label can be drawn on first and then stuck to the finger, if preferred. Hold the plate upright and insert fingers through the slit of the plate for an instant puppet theatre. You can make puppets on Popsicle sticks, tongue depressors, coffee stir sticks, or straws instead of fingers, if preferred.

Lighted Box Puppet Stage

Materials: cardboard boxes, two the same size; pencil, ruler, scissors, paint and brushes, masking and regular tape, flashlight.

Select one box. Cut away the top flaps and save for scraps. Draw a stage opening on the front of the box, making a rectangle from the base approximately two-thirds of the way up. Make the opening fairly large, but leave some room on the sides to keep the stage sturdy. Cut out the pieces (may need adult help). Paint the box inside and out with any chosen colors. Add painted decorations around the stage opening, if desired. Paint a sign for the puppet stage, like "Theatre Magnificent," "Puppet Show," or "Eric's Best Stage Shows." Let dry completely. When dry, cut lighting holes in the sides of the theatre. During a show, shine a flashlight through the holes to spotlight a puppet. You can cover the flashlight with colored cellophane held in place by a rubber band to change the lighting to different colors and effects. A lighted show may take two or more people to perform.

With cardboard from the second box and flap scraps, draw and paint scenery for the puppet stage. When dry, cut the scenery out with adult help. Depending on the store, the scenery might include a cottage, trees, or the inside of a house. The scenery will hang from the sticks into the stage area. Tape the top of each piece of scenery onto a long thing stick. Make each stick longer than the width of the box so it will rest on the top of the box. Cut little nicks in the left and right top edges of the box for the sticks to rest in so the scenery hangs down into the stage area.

Painted Hand Puppet

Materials: face paints such as Bicolor (use nontoxic paints that peel or wash off easily), brushes, markers (water-based and nontoxic), any puppet theatre, soap, water, old towel, old shirt (optional), rubber band or tape (optional), scissors (optional).

Experiment first with markers and paints to see how they work on skin. Then wash off paint and marker lines. Dry. Decide whether to make each finger into a puppet, making five puppets, or to make the entire hand into one puppet. With markers or paints, decorate fingers or hand as a puppet. See how the hand can be a full-face view or a side view. Notice how each finger can be a different character. To dress the hand puppet, create a "Sleeve Costume" by cutting the sleeve off an old shirt and secure it with a rubber band or piece of tape around the wrist. The sleeve will end near the elbow. Put on a show with any puppet theatre. When done, wash hands in soapy water and dry with an old towel. Sometimes paints can take a day or two to completely wear off.

Puppeteer

Materials: sofa or table, tablecloth and chairs, or 2 straight-backed chairs, a book, a clothesline or rope, and a blanket or sheet, puppets, and props.

There are three ways to make a stage. If there's room behind a sofa, you can hide back there and ask the audience to sit in front of it on the floor. If you have props and scenery you want to use, you'll need a stage with a real floor. A table works well—just pull a tablecloth down long enough to hide behind. The audience can sit on the opposite side of the table, where they won't be able to see you. If you want to build a simple puppet theatre yourself, take a pair of straight-backed chairs and place them a few feet away from each other. Tie a piece of clothesline or rope between them and set a few heavy books in each chair for balance. Then hang a blanket or sheet from the clothesline to make a curtain.

Lights, puppets, action. Send your puppets out on stage and give your show. Remember to use different voices for all the puppets, and move the one who's talking a little bit, so the audience can follow the action. Your show can be as simple or as complex as you want it to be. One or two puppets can sing a song or two, or you can use a crowd of them to tell a long, fanciful story. You can work by yourself behind the stage, or you can use as many other co-puppeteers as will fit behind your stage.

Sock Puppet

Materials: old sock, needle and thread or fabric glue, materials for decorating such as beads, buttons, felt scraps, fringes, googly craft eyes, masking tape, old jewelry, pompoms, rickrack, rug scraps, stick-on dots, yarn.

Pull the sock over the non-drawing hand, positioning the heel of the sock over the thumb. See how the puppet "talks" as the thumb and other fingers are pulled together and apart. Decide how to decorate the puppet making good use of the mouth of the sock puppet in the design. Begin sewing or gluing on scraps and other materials to give the puppet eyes, nose, hair, and personality. When done, help the puppet talk by opening and closing the puppet's mouth with a hand inside the sock.
More ideas: Stuff the toe of a sock with a ball of cotton stuffing or tissue paper. Tie a piece of string around the neck (not too tight) The rest of the sock is the puppets body. Glue or sew on decorations as desired. Insert fingers in the head of the puppet.
As with all puppets, make up an original story or act out a favorite book or fairy tale. Puppets can sing along with a favorite recording.

Stick Puppets

Materials: thing wooden sticks such as dowels, long bamboo skewers, or wooden gardener's stakes, pencil, file cards, scissors, glue, crayons or markers, paper clips, tape.

Sports, Recreation, & Arts

Draw and color puppets on file cards. Cut them out. Trace the puppets on a second file card and color these for the backs of puppets. Glue each front and back of the puppet to a stick. Be sure the stick comes out of the puppet's head upward. Hold until the glue sticks. Tape an opened paper clip to the top of the stick to work as a hook and a handle. You can hang the puppets when they are not moving but must remain on stage, on the scenery hooks in the puppet theatre. You can also attach small toys or other items such as toy cars, animals, dinosaurs, or doll furniture on the sticks to use as puppets or props.

Topical signs to be learned: puppet, hand, box, glue, crayon, pencil, scissors, paint, decorate, audience, perform, face, eye, nose, smile, person, animal, elephant, sock, stick, soap, wash, dry, light.

Presto! Magic Wand (fine & performing arts)

Materials: sturdy stick or dowel about 1 foot long, fabric glue, ten 6-inch strips of colored ribbon or fabric and another that's 2 inches long, sequins, pom-poms, feathers, or other decorations.

Use the stick or dowel as the handle for the wand. One end will be for holding, and the other end will be decorated with ribbons. Make sure you have 10 strips of ribbon or fabric, about 6 inches long and about an inch wide. Lay the wand down on newspaper or a work surface that glue won't ruin. Smear a small amount of glue on one end of the ribbon, and attach the glue side of the ribbon to the top of the wand. continue gluing all the pieces of the ribbon around the top of the wand. Make sure you place the ribbon at the same point on the stick, all the way around, so that you have an even edge. Let the wand sit for about 20 minutes, or until it's dry. Turn the wand upside down, so that the streamers are hanging away from the stick. Smear glue all over the 2-inch piece of ribbon or fabric and wrap it around the top of the wand. This creates a border on top of where the other ribbons are glued. Let the wand dry for 20 minutes. Turn the wand back upright and the ribbons will fall back over the wand like a waterfall. Glue decorations onto the ribbon or fabric that will glitter or move when you turn the wand. Make a wish!

Topical signs to be learned: glue, ribbon, dry, make, wish, decorations.

Recorder (fine & performing arts)

Materials: Paper towel tube, cone shaped drinking cup, aluminum foil, tape, circle shapes (either stickers or cut out circles), scissors.

Have the children cover the tubes with foil. Then create a mouthpiece out of foil, being sure to leave an opening on both ends of the mouthpiece. Insert one end of the tube, being sure it is snug and then glue or tape it into position. Cut off the pointed end of the cone shaped cup, then cover the cone with foil. Insert it into the opposite end of the tube and affix with tape or glue. Arrange and affix five colored stickers in a row. After the recorder is complete, let the glue dry if necessary, then have the children pretend to play by blowing and pressing on the keys. Now we are ready to play. Compare the sounds each of the different recorder makes. Play the recorder to one of your classes favorite songs having half the class play the recorder, while the other half sign. Then switch and play the song again or play another class favorite.

Topical signs to be learned: music, song, horn, paper, drinking cup, circle, glue, scissors, colors, hear, share, please, thank you.

Scrolling Story Box

Materials: cardboard box, strong and medium sized; tape, scissors (or sharp knife for adult only), crayons, markers, long roll of butcher paper (or sheets of paper taped together to make a long roll), 2 wooden dowels about 12" long (or an old broomstick or paper towel tubes).

Cut a rectangular piece from the smooth side of a cardboard box for the viewing screen. Next cut two slits on the side ends of the box a little bigger than the paper width, about 12" x 2". Spread the roll of paper out on a table or smooth floor surface with the beginning edge at the right, and any extra paper to the left. Think of a story, book, fairy tale, song, or movie to draw. Draw the story on the roll of paper in a sequence of events, from the first thing that happens to the last thing that happens. When finished drawing the story, re-roll the paper onto a dowel or paper towel tube with the right edge (where the first pictures is) free. To prepare the drawings for a show, feed the paper from the left slit and across the viewing rectangle to the right slit. Pull it through and tape it to the second dowel or paper towel tube. Now the drawings are ready to scroll. Slowly roll the drawings from the left to the right onto the dowel. Tell the story out loud, or simply enjoy viewing the drawings. When finished, roll the drawings back onto the left dowel or paper towel tube. Add music or a story tape to enhance the show. The first "page" in the viewing window could be a title, design box, or sign.

Topical signs to be learned: box, scissors, paper, story, book, song, movie, draw, event, first, last, happen, finished, roll, tell, title.

Stilts (sports & recreation)

Materials: 2 pieces of 6-8' long 2"x2" lumber, 2"x4" pieces of wood, screws; OR medium sized tin cans (such as soup cans), sharp object to punch holes, small rope or stout cord.

For wooden stilts, screw the 2"x4" pieces of wood into the larger pieces of wood. Place the "platforms" lower for beginning stilt walkers. Walking on stilts is simply fun and is reward enough. Racing is too hazardous.
For tin can stilts, punch two holes in the bottom rim of each can, large enough to admit the stout cord or small rope. The cards are grasped tightly in each hand to hold the cans against the feet. Thus one can walk fairly rapidly but precariously.

Topical signs to be learned: big, little, walk, fun, careful.

Superstar Iced Cookies (fine & performing arts)

Materials: large mixing bowl, electric mixer, sifter, medium-sized bowl, wooden spoon, star-shaped cookie cutter or table knife, rolling pin, cookie sheets, wire

Sports, Recreation, & Arts

cooling racks, small mixing bowl, spoon, pot holders, 1 stick (8 tablespoons) unsalted butter at room temperature, 1 cup sugar, 2 cups sifted all-purpose flour, ¼ teaspoon salt, ½ teaspoon baking powder, 1 large egg lightly beaten, ½ teaspoon vanilla extract, 1 ½ cups powdered sugar, ½ teaspoon vanilla extract, 6 tablespoons water.

Put the butter and sugar into a large mixing bowl. Using an electric mixer on low to medium speed, cream them together until the mixture is smooth. Sift together flour, salt, and baking powder (the dry ingredients) into a medium-sized bowl. Add the dry ingredients to the butter/sugar mixture. Stir with a wooden spoon or with the mixer on low until everything blends together. Add the eggs and vanilla, and combine until well mixed. Chill dough in the refrigerator for 1 hour. Preheat oven to 350 degrees F. Lightly flour a rolling pin and flat area on the kitchen counter. Working carefully, roll the dough 1/8 inch thick. Cut the dough into star shapes with a cookie cutter or table knife. Then put them on baking sheets, so that they're at least ½ inch apart. Bake the cookies for approximately 10 minutes. Do not let them brown. Using pot holders, remove the baking sheets from the oven and place the cookies on wire racks to cool.

Making the Icing
In a small bowl, use a spoon to blend together the powdered sugar, vanilla extract, and water until the mixture is smooth. Add more water if the icing is too thick to spread. Frost the cookies. Feel free to lick the bowl when you're through. After all, you're the star!

Topical signs to be learned: bowl, spoon, butter, sugar, eggs, smooth, salt, bake, star, shape, roll, water, smooth.

Textured Crayon Pictures (fine & performing arts)
Materials: crayons, paper, glue, decorating materials such as fabric, sponges, cotton, ribbon or string, felt, sticks, paper, beans or seeds, glitter, beads, etc.

Draw a picture with crayons, and when finished use as many materials as possible to give texture to it. Clothes can be real fabrics glued on, but avoid porous materials such as linen, which shows the glue. Trees or bushes could be covered with tiny bits of green craft paper, glued over another like shingles. String or yarn can be used for a kite's tale and string. The possibilities for ingenuity are almost unlimited.

Topical signs to be learned: texture, crayon, draw, glue, paper, string, ribbon, decorate, clothes, tree, string, kite.

Textured Painting (fine & performing arts)
Materials: sawdust, poster paint, cardboard, pencil, paste or glue, paint or crayons (optional), coffee ground or sand (optional).

Dye the sawdust (any except redwood or cedar) the color desired by covering with poster paint. When the color has soaked in, drain sawdust on newspaper and dry. Draw the outlines of a picture on a cardboard back. Then spread paste or glue on all the areas that are to be a certain color. When dry, paste over the areas of another color, and repeat until the textured area has been covered color by color. For better contrast cover only part of the picture with sawdust; perhaps just the figure, in front of a painted or crayon-colored background. In this case, do the textured part last. Experiment by adding dried coffee grounds or sand, plus a little glue, to small quantities of poster paints, if desired.

Topical signs to be learned: texture, paint, pencil, glue, paint, crayon, draw, color signs, dry.

Three Sculpting Dough Recipes (fine & performing arts)
Basic Breadcraft (excellent flour and salt dough)
Materials: 4 cups flour, 1 cup salt, 1 cup water (plus more), mixing bowl, tempera paint or food color (optional), foil or waxed paper, paint and brushes (optional).

Combine 4 cups flour and 1 cup salt in a bowl. Make a well in the center and pour in 1 cup water. Mix with hands. Add up to ½ cup more water and continue mixing by hand. Dough should form a ball but not be crumbly or sticky. Knead five minutes on a floured board until smooth. If desired, knead in tempera paint or food coloring for color. Work with small portions of dough on foil or wax paper. Bake for one hour at 325 degrees F until hard. Then cool. Can be painted when cool.

Funclay (smooth white dough, dries in several hours)
Materials: 2 cups salt, 1 cup water, 1 cup cornstarch, pan, bowl, mixing spoon, waxed paper, tempera paint or food color (optional), paint and brushes (optional).

Mix 2 cups salt and 2/3 cup water in a pan. Bring to a boil. Mix 1 cup cornstarch and 1/3 cup cold water in a bowl. Mix cornstarch mixture into the salt mixture. Cool. Knead on waxed paper until dough-like. Knead in tempera paint or food coloring, if desired. Now sculpt and model with the clay. Remember to pull out clay to make arms, heads, and legs rather than sticking separate pieces on. Dries in several hours. Can be painted when dry.

Basic Play Clay (white and hard, dries quickly)
Materials: 1 cup baking soda, ½ cup cornstarch, 2/3 cup water, pan, food coloring or paint (optional), nail polish or clear hobby coating.

Mix baking soda and cornstarch in pan. Add about 2/3 cup water and stir until smooth. Cook over medium heat. Boil until like mashed potatoes. Pour on a board to cool. Then knead. Add color to the dough with drops of food coloring or paint, if desired. Sculpt and model clay. Let dry for an hour or so. Paint, if desired. For a protective coating, paint with nail polish or any clear hobby coating.

Topical signs to be learned: salt, water, cup, measure, bowl, paint, food color, paint, pour, ball, bake, cold, dry.

Waxed Garfield (fine & performing arts)
Materials: comic strips (preferably through not essentially in color), waxed paper, spoon.

Sports, Recreation, & Arts

Place a piece of waxed paper over a picture from the comic pages (or a comic book). Using the edge (not the rounded base) of a spoon, rub over the picture. Be sure to rub all of the picture. Don't rub over anything you don't want to capture on the waxed paper or you'll have inadvertently included a tree, half a person, or the edge of the next panel. Rub firmly, though be careful not to tear the paper. Remember that whatever you pick up will come out reversed. With a little practice, you'll eventually be ready to make composite strips. You can create quite a menagerie of comic strip canines and felines...or a playground full of comic strip kids, or any other sort of composite you want.

Topical signs to be learned: paper, picture, spoon.

Water Bells (fine & performing arts)
Materials: 8 clear 6" high water glasses, water, 2 metal spoons, numbered cards from 1-8.

Line up the 8 glasses in a row, close together, but not touching. Place the numbers in front of the glasses in order from 1-8. Add water to the glasses as follows:

½ inch in glass 1	3 ½ inches in glass 5
1 ¼ inches in glass 2	4 ¼ inches in glass 6
2 inches in glass 3	5 inches in glass 7
2 ¾ inches in glass 4	5 ¾ inches in glass 8

Now we are ready to play. Compare the sounds each of the different glass bell makes. Play the glass bells to one of your classes favorite songs having half the class play some of their other instrument creations, while the other half sign (all sing). Then switch instruments and take turns playing the glass bells to other familiar favorites

Topical signs to be learned: Music, song, water, glass, measurement, hear, share, please, thank you.

Fine & Performing Arts Signs

-

Señales de Artes Interpretativas

Sports, Recreation, & Arts   51

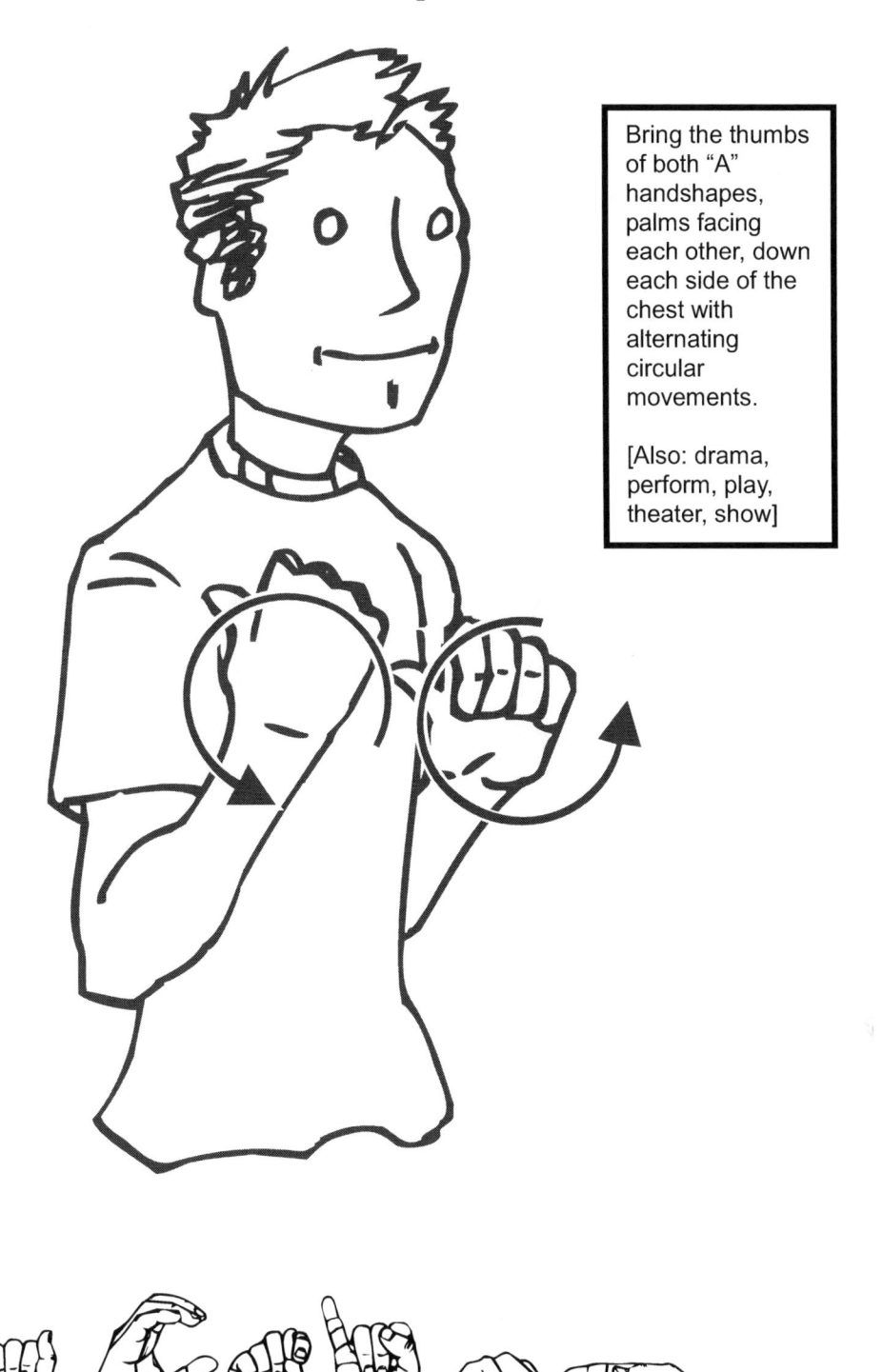

Bring the thumbs of both "A" handshapes, palms facing each other, down each side of the chest with alternating circular movements.

[Also: drama, perform, play, theater, show]

acting - actuación

Sports, Recreation, & Arts

Move the extended dominant little finger, palm facing in, with a wiggly movement down the palm of the reference open hand, palm facing forward, from the fingers to the heel.

[Also: drawing, illustration, sketch.]

art – arte

Sports, Recreation, & Arts

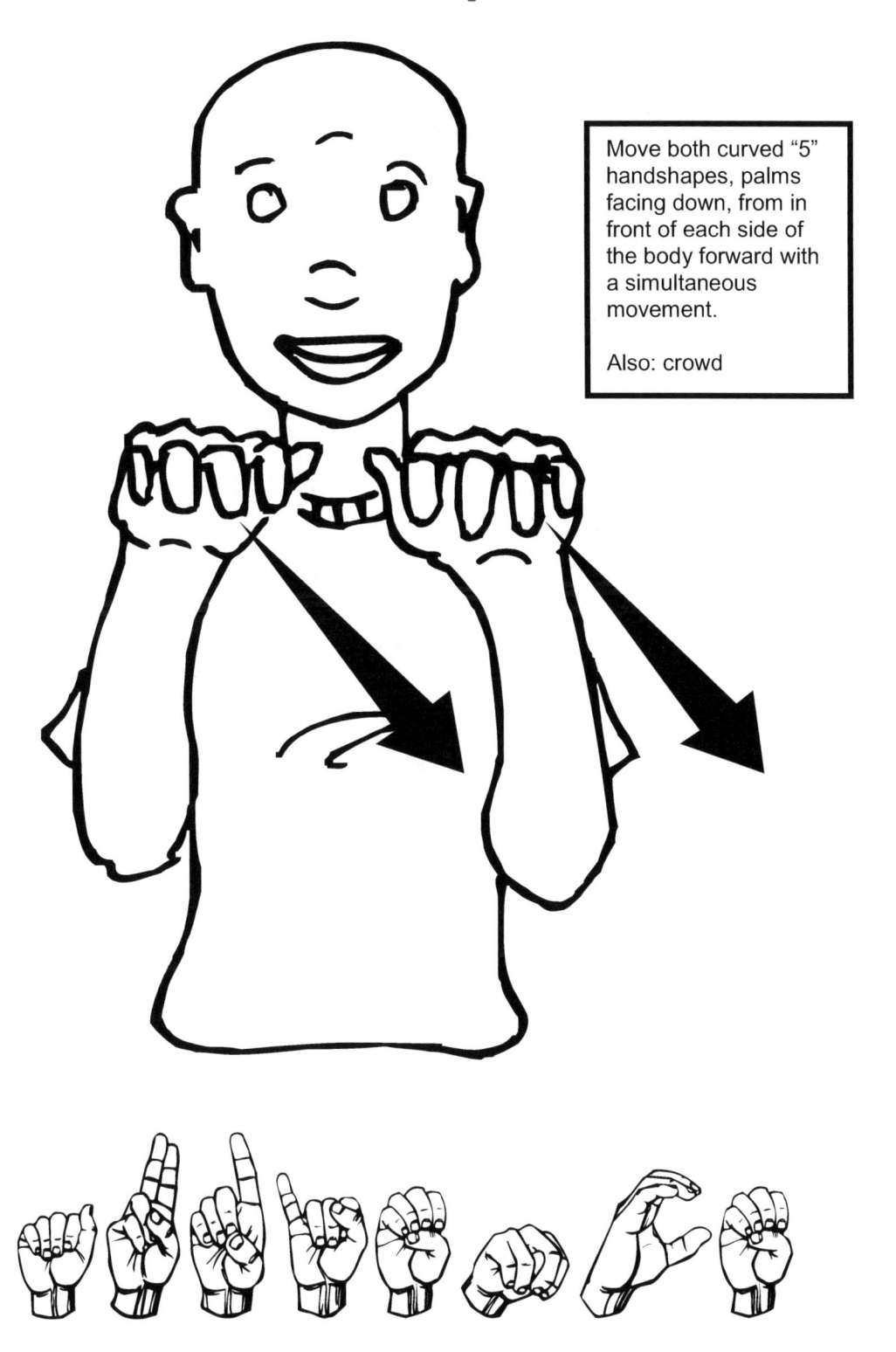

> Move both curved "5" handshapes, palms facing down, from in front of each side of the body forward with a simultaneous movement.
>
> Also: crowd

audience - audiencia

Move the dominant open "5" handshape, palm facing in, back and forth with a double movement across the length of the bent reference forearm held in front of the body, palm facing up. Then place both hands in front of the body, palms facing forward, draw them apart to the side and around to the front until the little fingers touch.

[Sign: music + class]

band - banda

Sports, Recreation, & Arts

> Move the index finger side of the dominant "B" handshape from the wrist to near the elbow of the bent reference arm.

basket - canasta

Sports, Recreation, & Arts

Start with the dominant "5" handshape in front of the face, palm facing in, move in a circular movement, closing the fingers and the thumb in front of the chin to form a flattened "O" handshape.

beauty – belleza

Sports, Recreation, & Arts 57

Begin with the forearm of the dominant "S" handshape, palm facing forward, against the thumb side of the reference "B" handshape, palm facing down and fingers pointing toward the dominant side, bend the dominant arm downward while bending the body forward.

[Also: bend, nod.]

bow - reverencia

Begin with the modified "C" handshapes near the outside of each eye, palms facing each other, bend the dominant index finger up and down with a repeated movement.

[Mimics taking a picture with a camera]

camera – cámara

Sports, Recreation, & Arts   59

> Move the thumb of the dominant "C" handshape in a wavy motion from the heel to the fingertips of the reference open hand, palm facing up.

crayon – crayola

Sports, Recreation, & Arts

Begin with the dominant "C" handshape, palm facing reference side, near the extended reference index finger, palm facing dominant side, move the dominant hand in a circle forward and around the reference index finger. Then move the extended dominant little finger, palm facing reference, with a wiggly movement down the palm of the reference open hand from the thumb to the little finger side.

cultural art – arte cultural

Sports, Recreation, & Arts   61

Swing the fingers of the dominant "V" handshape, palm facing in and fingers pointing down, back and forth over the upturned reference hand with a double movement.

[As if dancing with the fingers]

dance – bailar

Sports, Recreation, & Arts

Move the extended dominant little finger, palm facing reference, with a wiggly movement down the palm of the reference open hand from the thumb to the little finger side.

draw – dibujar

Sports, Recreation, & Arts   63

> Move both modified "X" handshapes, palms facing in and knuckles pointing toward each other, up and down in front of the chest with a repeated alternating movement.
>
> [Mimics playing a drum]

drum – tambor

Begin with the "5" handshape in front of the face, palm facing in, open fingers and circle the hand in front of the face. Then change to a flattened "O" handshape and end in an open "5" handshape. Then move the extended dominant little finger, palm facing reference, with a wiggly movement down the palm of the reference open hand from the thumb to the little finger side.

fine art – las bellas artes

Sports, Recreation, & Arts   65

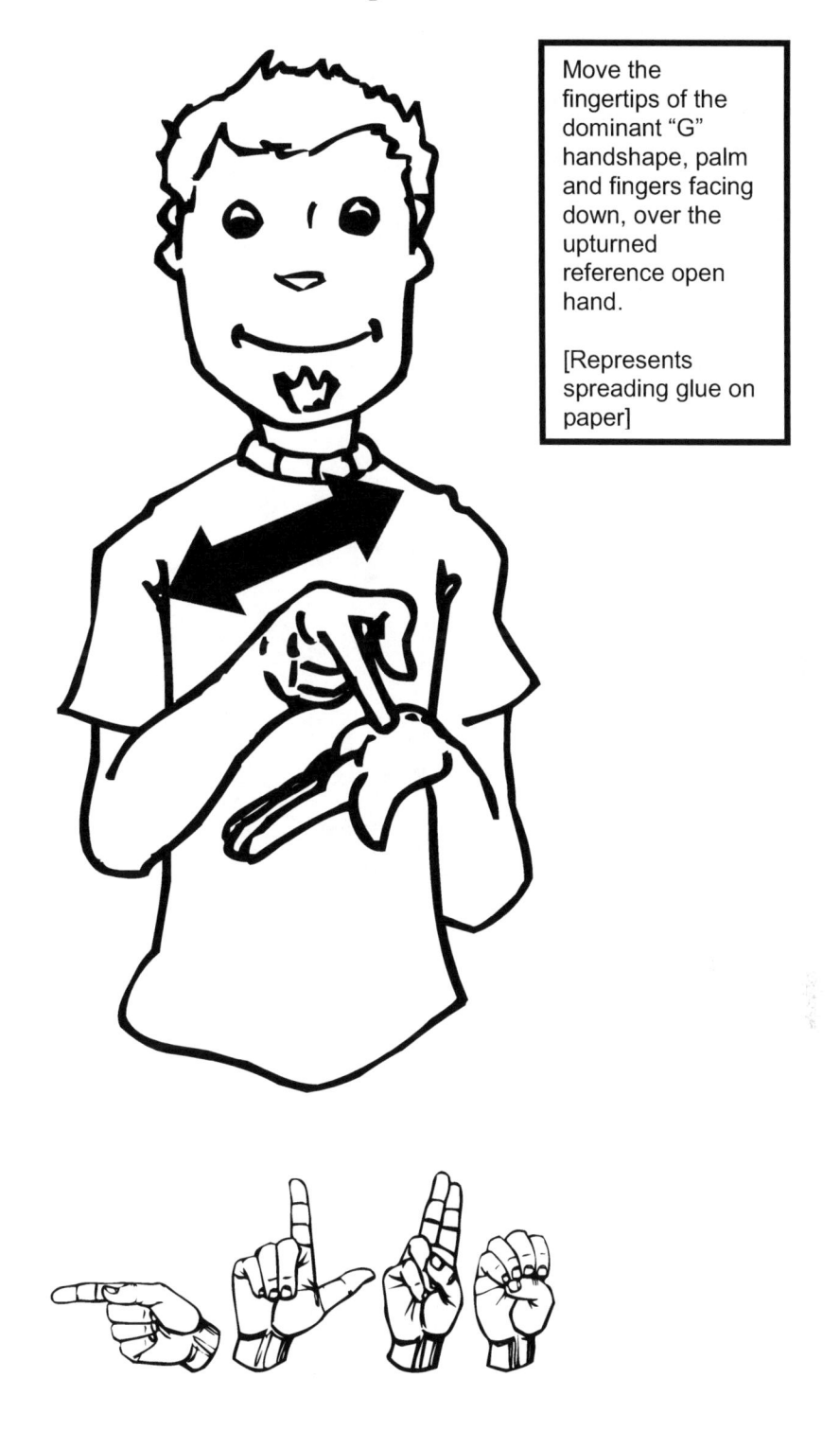

> Move the fingertips of the dominant "G" handshape, palm and fingers facing down, over the upturned reference open hand.
>
> [Represents spreading glue on paper]

glue – cola, pegar

Copyright © 2005-2013 Time to Sign, Inc.

Sports, Recreation, & Arts

With the reference curved "5" handshape in front of the reference shoulder, palm facing dominant side, and the dominant "F" handshape in front of the dominant side of the body, palm facing body, twist the dominant hand downward with a double movement.

[Mimics playing a guitar with a pick]

guitar - guitarra

Sports, Recreation, & Arts   67

Hold the reference "S" handshape in front of the mouth, palm facing dominant side, and the dominant "C" handshape in front of the face, palm facing reference side.

[Mimics holding a horn and blowing into it]

horn – trompeta

Sports, Recreation, & Arts

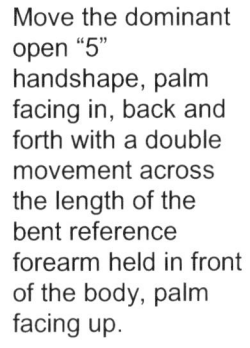

Move the dominant open "5" handshape, palm facing in, back and forth with a double movement across the length of the bent reference forearm held in front of the body, palm facing up.

[Also: song, sing]

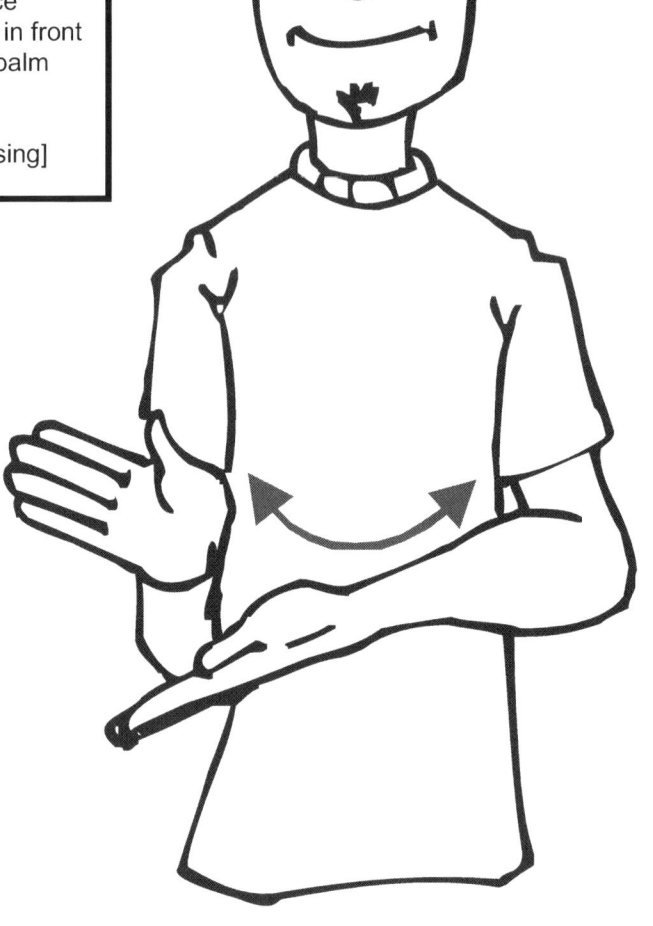

music – música

Sports, Recreation, & Arts   69

Bring the fingertips of the dominant open handshape down the length of the reference hand palm with a double movement, pulling the back of the dominant hand fingers up the reference hand palm to the fingertips each time.

[As if your dominant hand is painting the palm of your reference hand]

paint – pintura

Sweep the heel of the dominant "5" handshape, palm down, back against the heel of the upturned reference "5" handshape with an upward motion.

paper – papel

Sports, Recreation, & Arts 71

Bring the thumbs of both "A" handshapes, palms facing each other, down each side of the chest with alternating circular movements. Then move the extended dominant little finger with a wiggly movement down the palm of the reference open hand from the thumb to the little finger side.

[Sign: act + art]

performing art – artes interpretativas

Sports, Recreation, & Arts

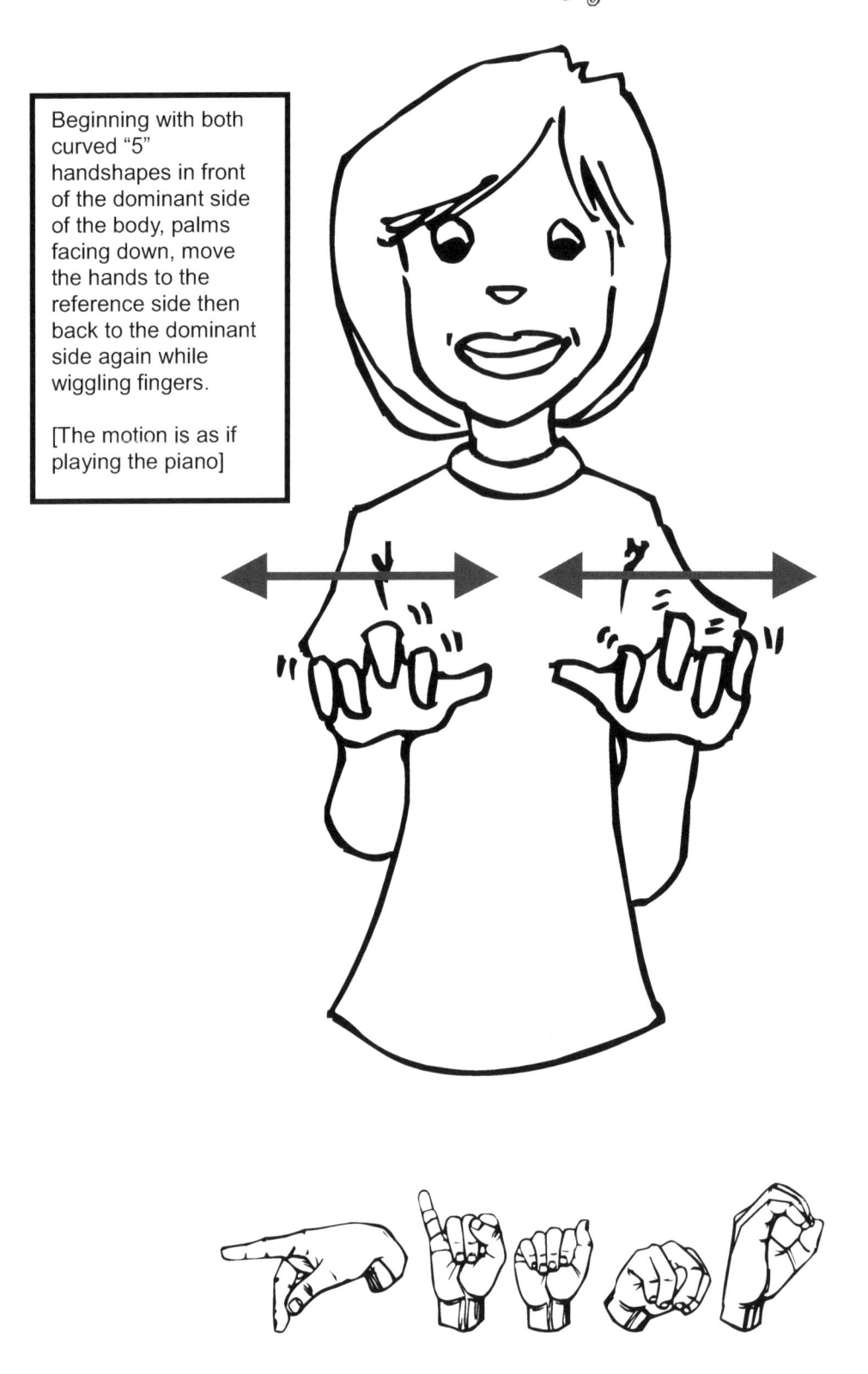

Beginning with both curved "5" handshapes in front of the dominant side of the body, palms facing down, move the hands to the reference side then back to the dominant side again while wiggling fingers.

[The motion is as if playing the piano]

piano – piano

Sports, Recreation, & Arts 73

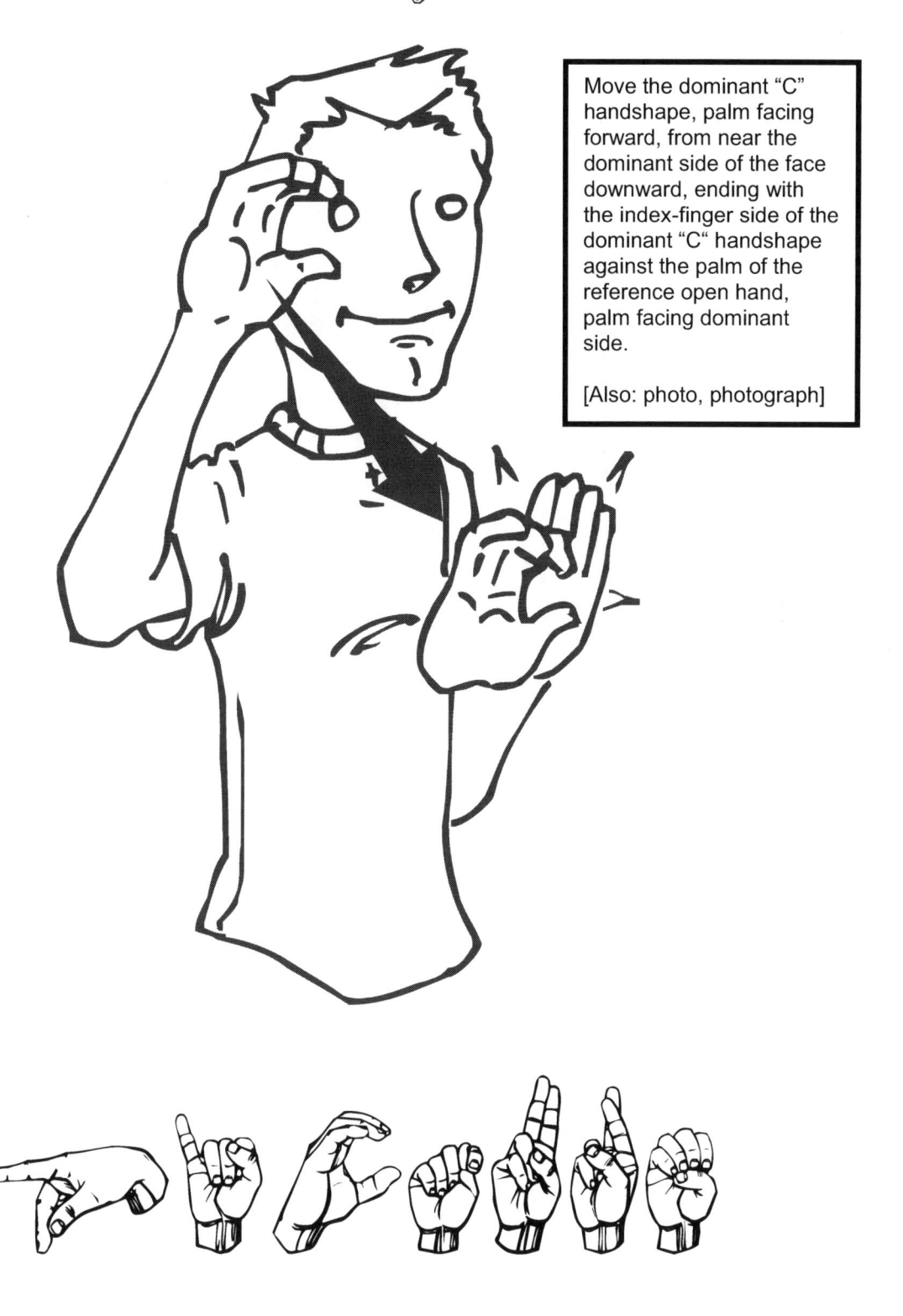

Move the dominant "C" handshape, palm facing forward, from near the dominant side of the face downward, ending with the index-finger side of the dominant "C" handshape against the palm of the reference open hand, palm facing dominant side.

[Also: photo, photograph]

picture - fotografía

Copyright © 2005-2013 Time to Sign, Inc.

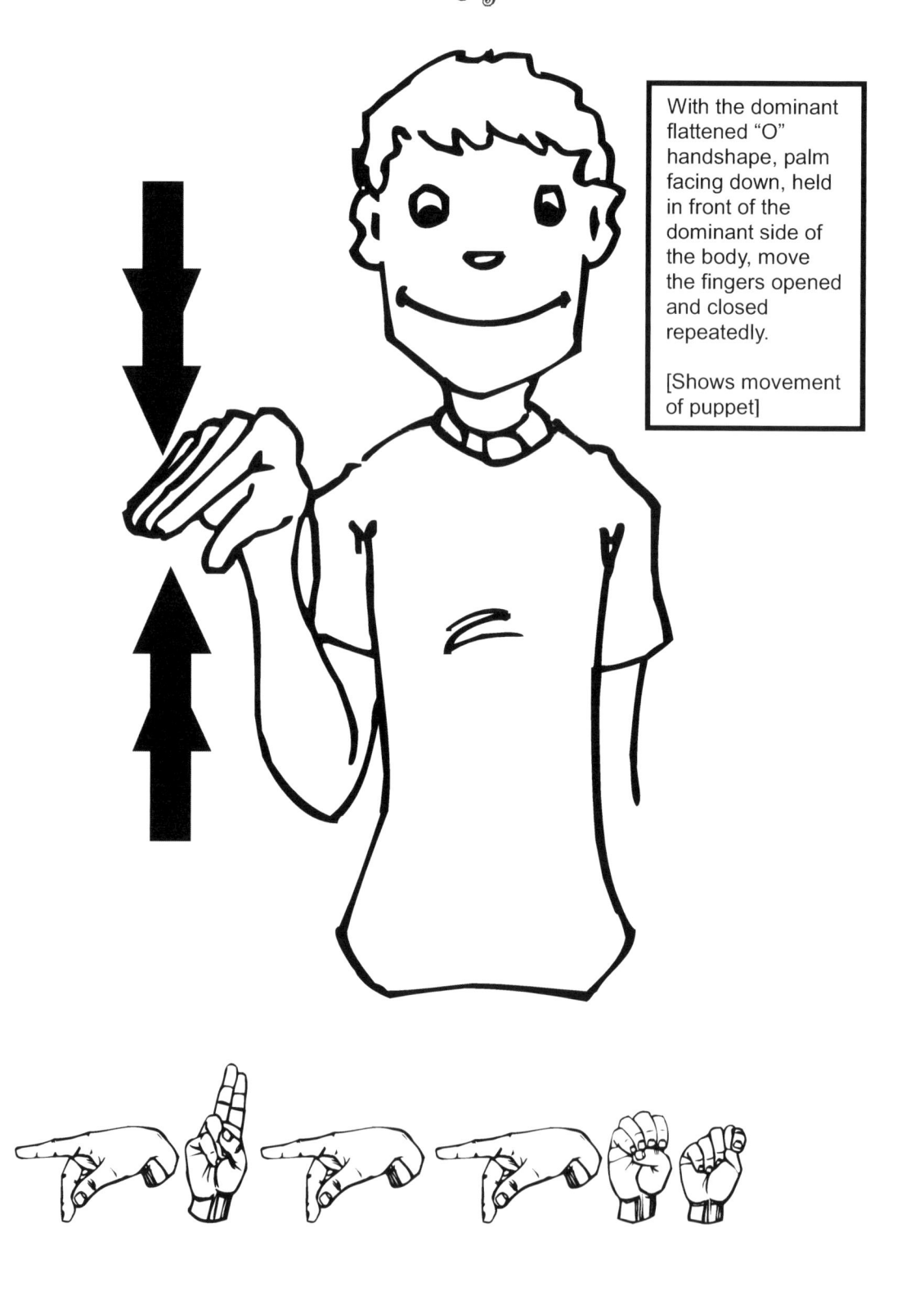

74   **Sports, Recreation, & Arts**

> With the dominant flattened "O" handshape, palm facing down, held in front of the dominant side of the body, move the fingers opened and closed repeatedly.
>
> [Shows movement of puppet]

puppet – títere

Sports, Recreation, & Arts 75

Open and close the index and middle fingers of the dominant "V" handshape, palm facing in and fingers pointing towards reference, with a repeated movement.

[Mimic cutting with scissors]

scissors – tijeras

76 Sports, Recreation, & Arts

Move the fingers of the dominant open hand, palm facing down, from the wrist of the fingertips across the top of the reference open hand held in front of the body, palm facing down.

smooth – liso

Sports, Recreation, & Arts 77

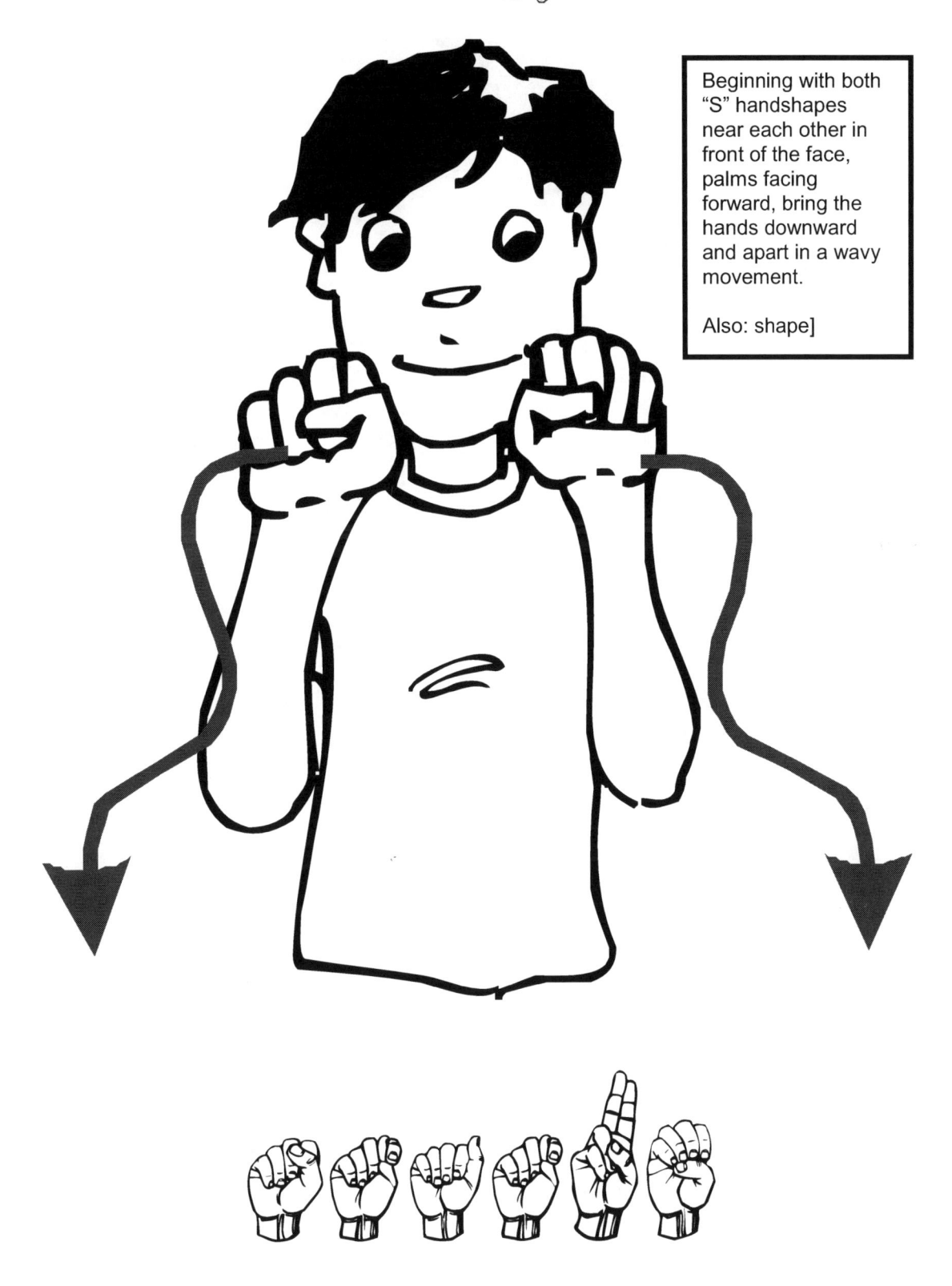

> Beginning with both "S" handshapes near each other in front of the face, palms facing forward, bring the hands downward and apart in a wavy movement.
>
> Also: shape]

statue – estatua

Grasp the little finger side of the reference open hand with the curved dominant fingers. Then pull the dominant hand forward while closing the fingers into the palm.

[Also: skill, ability, expert]

talent – talento

Sports, Recreation, & Arts   79

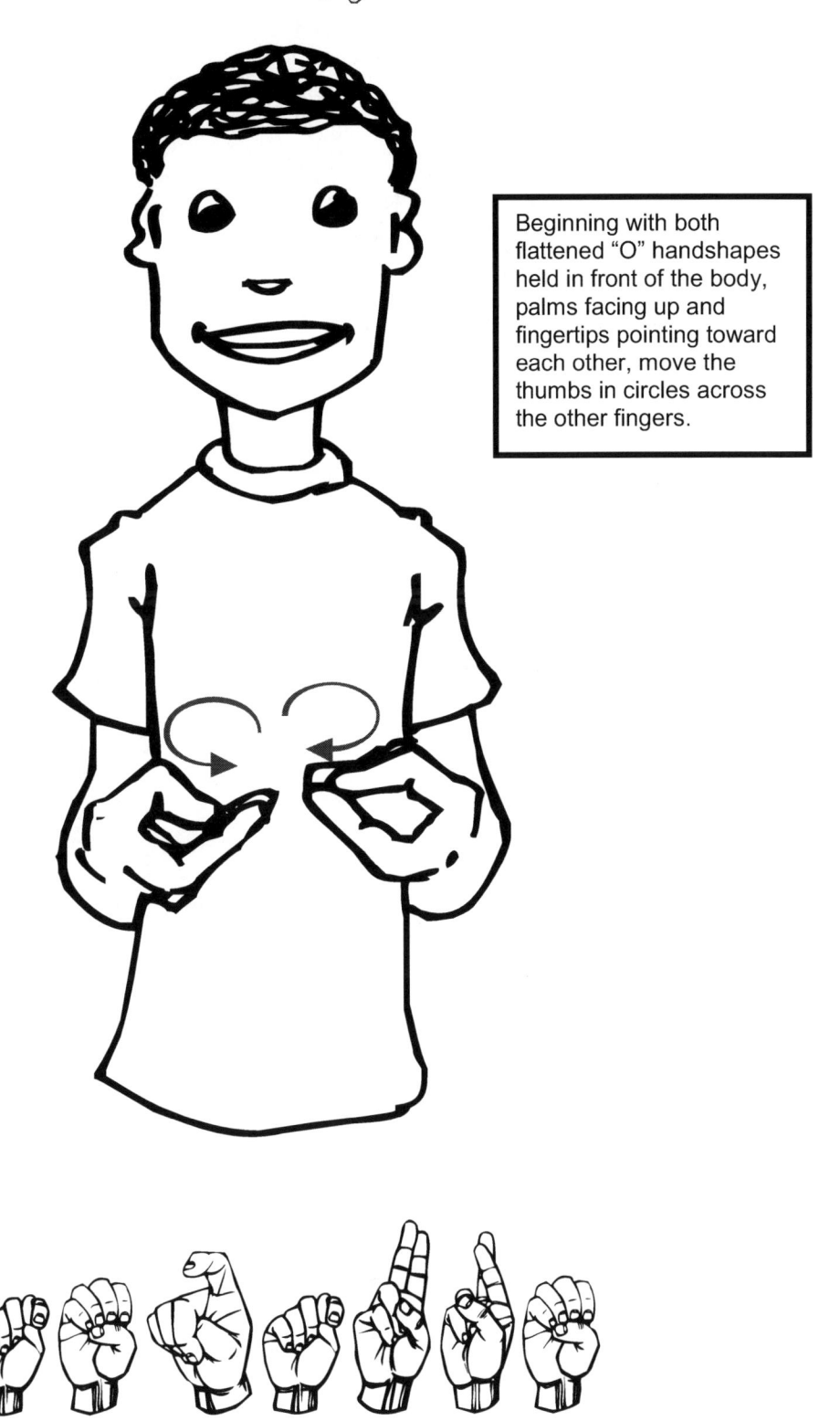

> Beginning with both flattened "O" handshapes held in front of the body, palms facing up and fingertips pointing toward each other, move the thumbs in circles across the other fingers.

texture - textura

Sports, Recreation, & Arts

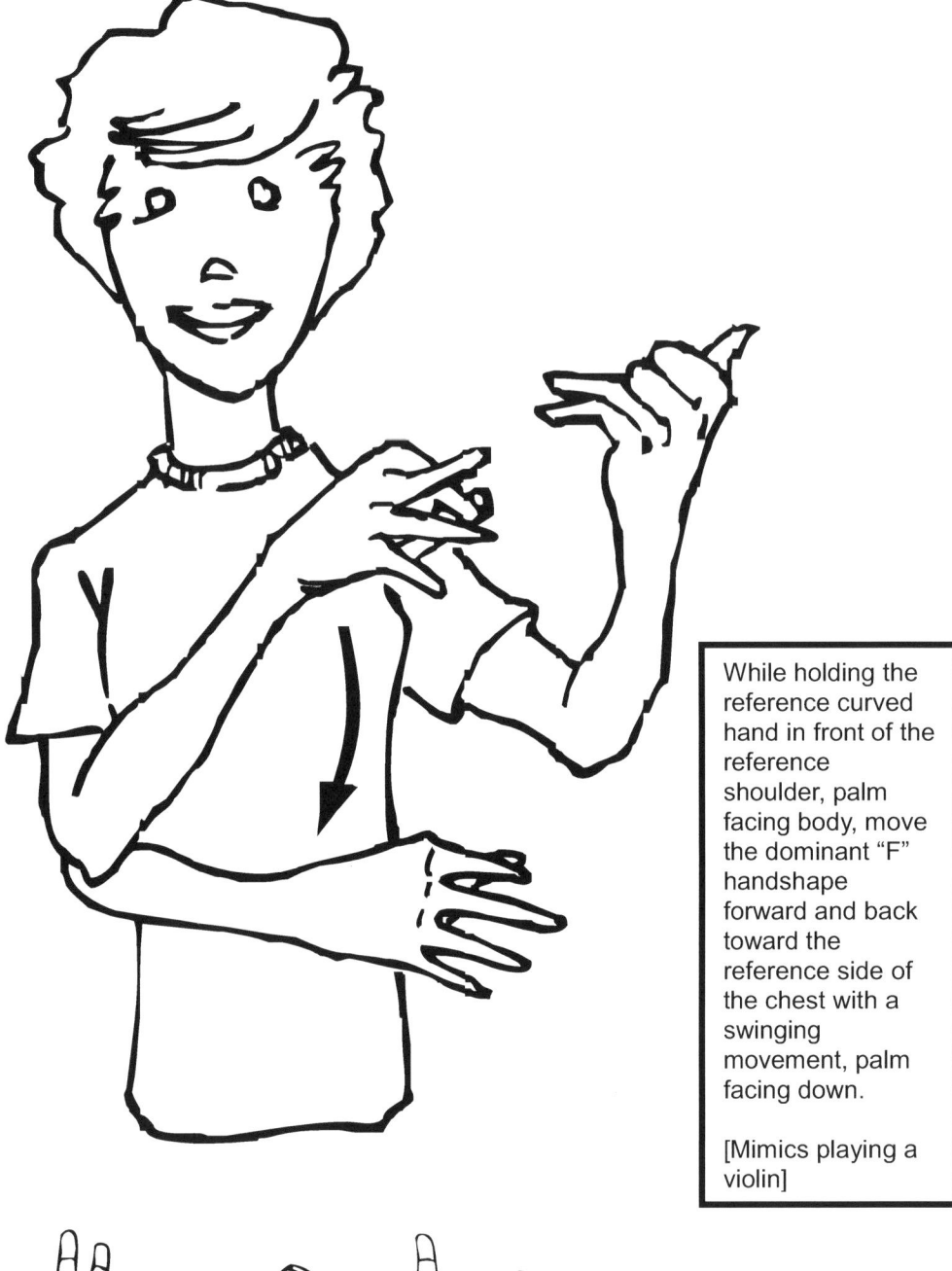

While holding the reference curved hand in front of the reference shoulder, palm facing body, move the dominant "F" handshape forward and back toward the reference side of the chest with a swinging movement, palm facing down.

[Mimics playing a violin]

violin - violín

Sports, Recreation, & Arts

81

Begin with the palms of both modified "X" handshapes facing each other in front of each side of the body, move the hands up and down with an alternating movement.

[Mimics playing a xylophone.]

xylophone - xilófono

Sports and Recreation Signs

-

Señales de Deportes y Recreo

Sports, Recreation, & Arts 83

Move the thumbs of both curved "3" handshapes, palms facing forward, downward toward each shoulder with a double movement.

backpack – mochila

84   Sports, Recreation, & Arts

Touch the fingertips of both curved "5" handshape together in front of the chest, palms facing inward.

[Indicates holding a ball in your hands]

ball – pelota

Sports, Recreation, & Arts 85

With the little finger of the dominant "S" hand on the index finger of the reference "S" hand, palms facing in opposite directions, move the hands from near the dominant shoulder downward in an arc across the front of the body.

[Natural gesture of swinging a baseball bat.]

baseball – béisbol

Sports, Recreation, & Arts

Move the curved "5" handshapes from in front of the chest, palms facing each other, upward with a double movement by twisting the wrists upward.

[Acting as if holding a basketball or playing with a basketball]

basketball – baloncesto

Sports, Recreation, & Arts 87

> Move both "S" handshapes in alternating forward circles, palms facing down, in front of each side of the body.
>
> [Mimics action of pedaling a bicycle]

bicycle – bicicleta

With the little finger sides of both curved hands together, palms facing up, move the hands forward in a bouncing double arc.

[Shows the shape of a boats hull]

boat – bote

Sports, Recreation, & Arts　　　　　　　　　　　　　　89

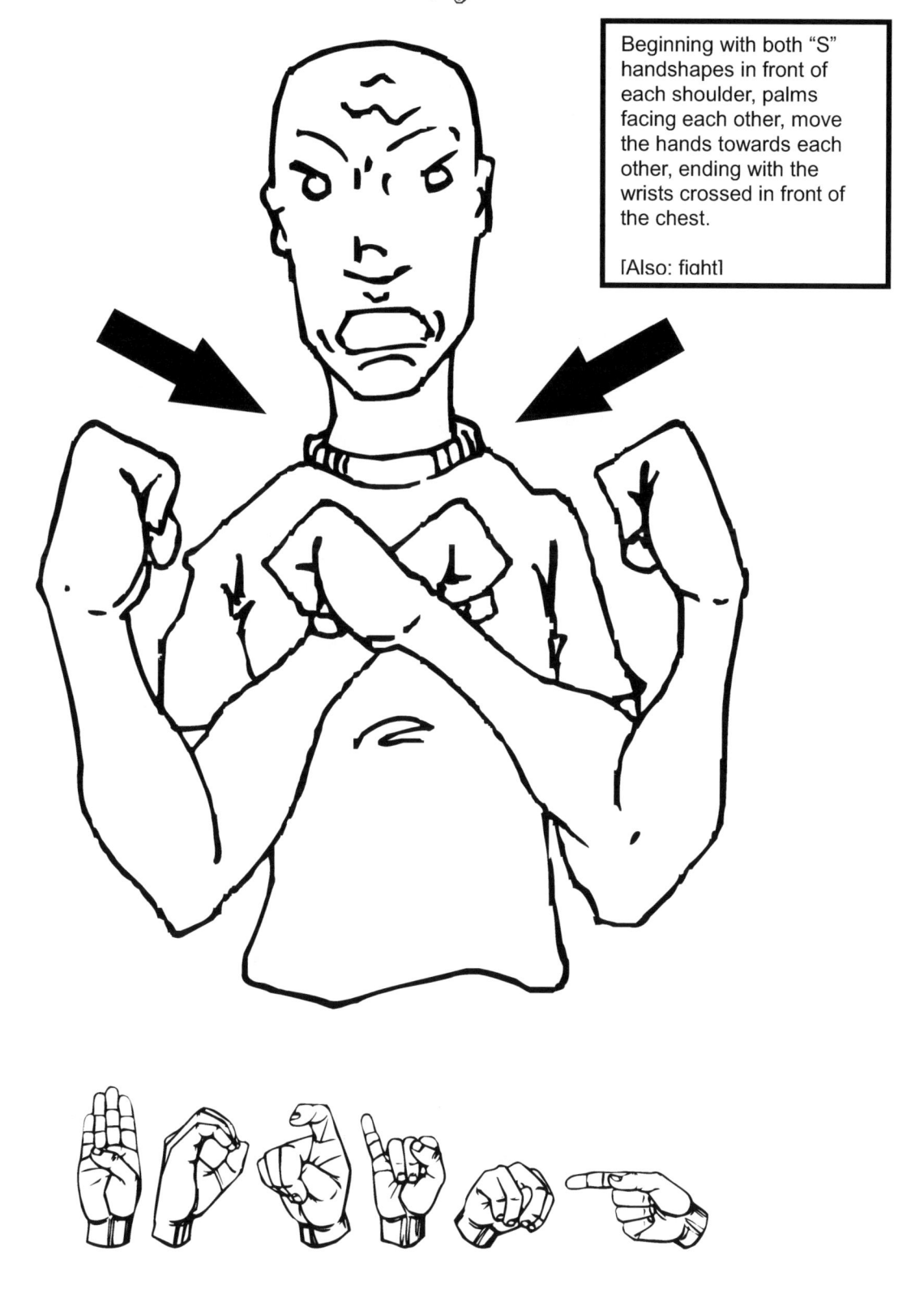

> Beginning with both "S" handshapes in front of each shoulder, palms facing each other, move the hands towards each other, ending with the wrists crossed in front of the chest.
>
> [Also: fight]

boxing – boxeo

Beginning with the extended index fingers and little fingers of both hands touching at an angle in front of the chest, bring the hands downward and apart with a repeated movement.

[Also: tent]

camp – acampar

Sports, Recreation, & Arts 91

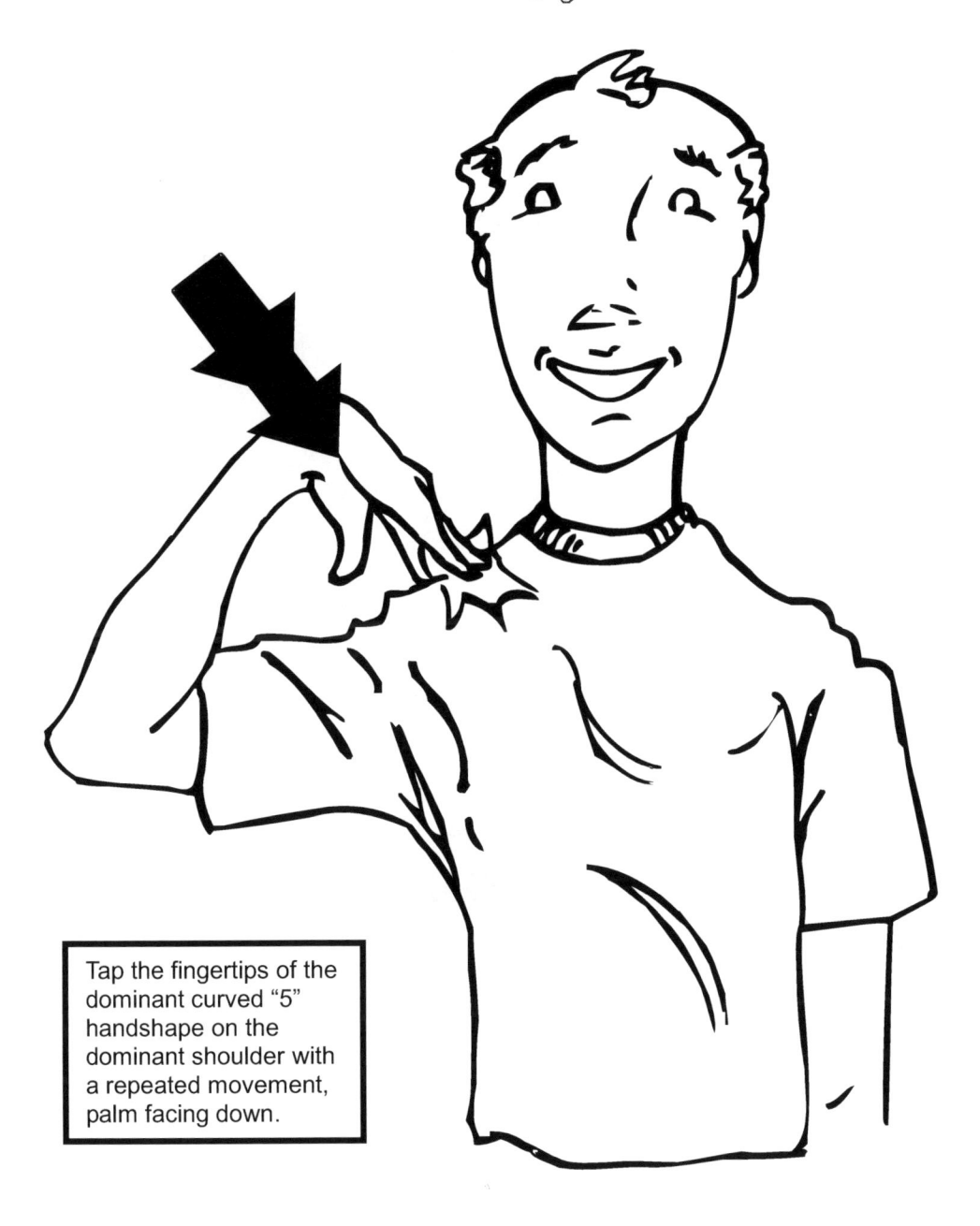

Tap the fingertips of the dominant curved "5" handshape on the dominant shoulder with a repeated movement, palm facing down.

captain - capitán

92 Sports, Recreation, & Arts

Beginning with both "S" handshapes in front of the chest, palms facing in and the reference hand higher than the dominant hand, move the hands in an up-and-down motion with a repeated alternating movement.

[Mimic driving a car]

car – coche, automóvil

Sports, Recreation, & Arts 93

> Move the dominant curved hand into the reference curved "5" hand in front of the chest.
>
> [Indicates receiving a ball into a glove.]

catch - coger

94 Sports, Recreation, & Arts

With the fingers of the dominant curved "3" handshape, tap the dominant palm on the extended reference index finger pointing up in front of the chest.

[Also: trophy]

champion – campeón

Sports, Recreation, & Arts 95

With both open "5" handshapes to the side of the body, palms facing out, shake hands with a repeated movement.

[Also: clapping in sign]

cheer – viva, aplausos

Sports, Recreation, & Arts

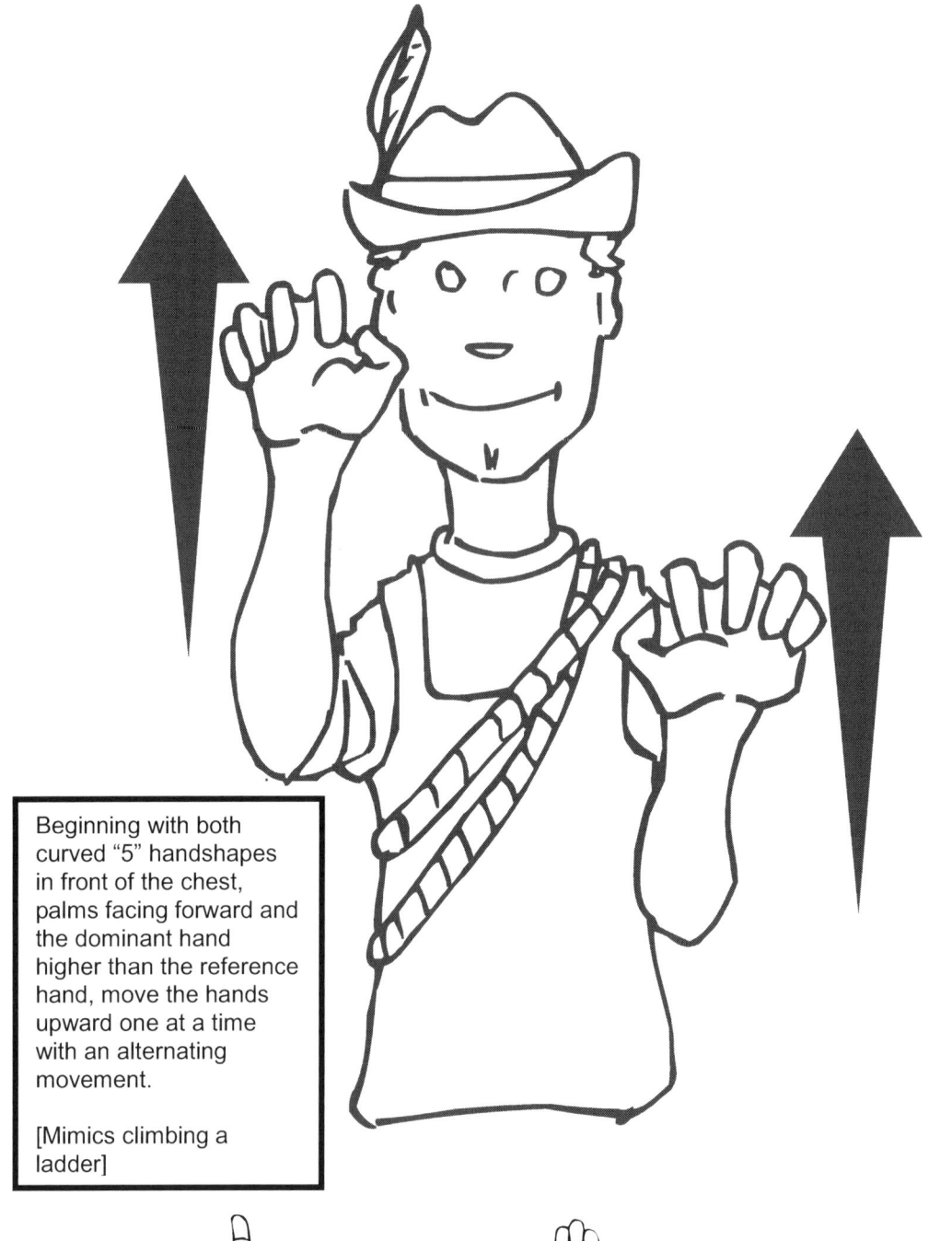

Beginning with both curved "5" handshapes in front of the chest, palms facing forward and the dominant hand higher than the reference hand, move the hands upward one at a time with an alternating movement.

[Mimics climbing a ladder]

climbing – escalar

Sports, Recreation, & Arts 97

> With an alternating movement, move both "A" handshapes forward and back past each other quickly, palms facing each other in front of the body.

competition - competencia

Sports, Recreation, & Arts

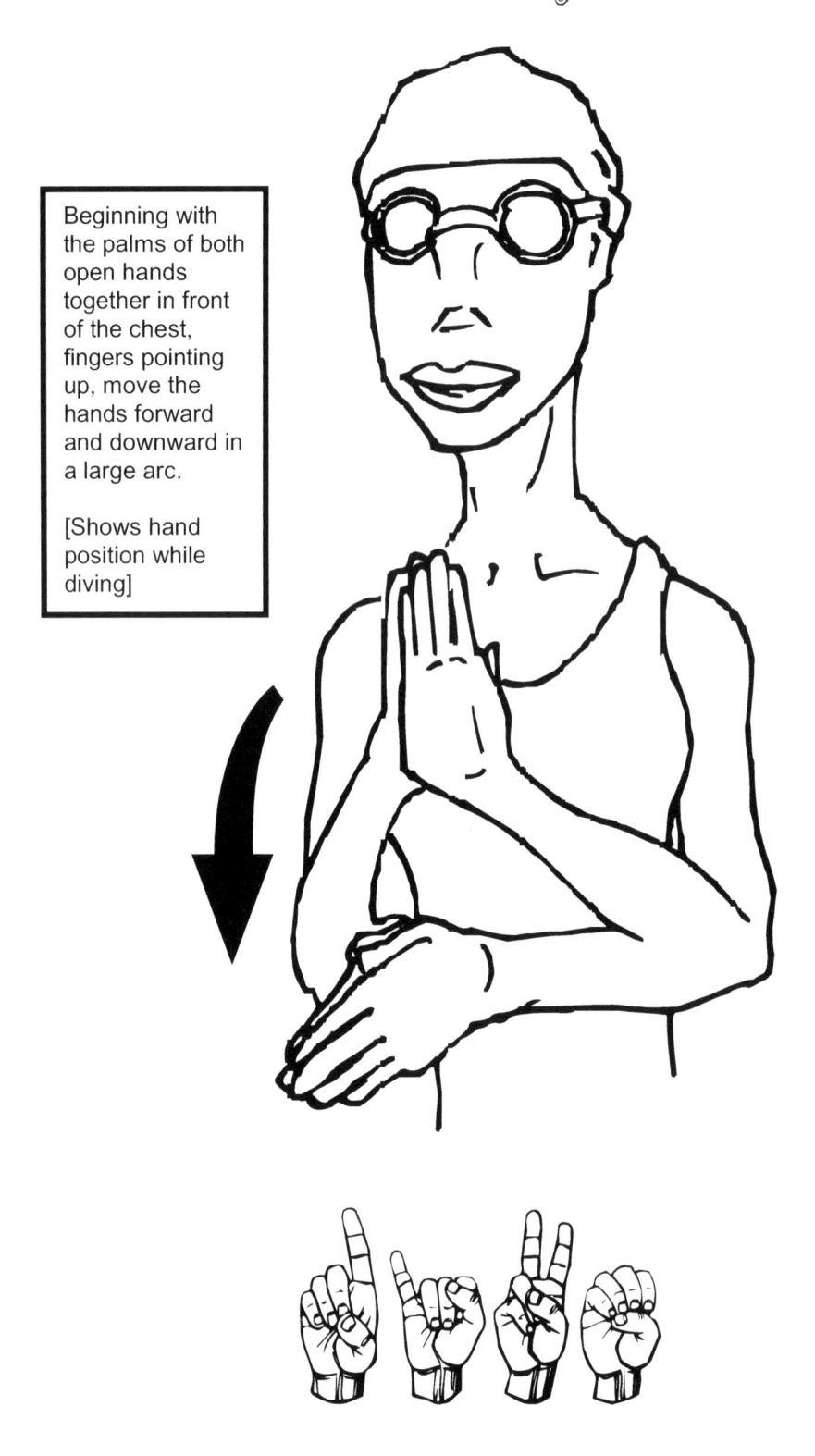

> Beginning with the palms of both open hands together in front of the chest, fingers pointing up, move the hands forward and downward in a large arc.
>
> [Shows hand position while diving]

dive – zambullirse

Sports, Recreation, & Arts

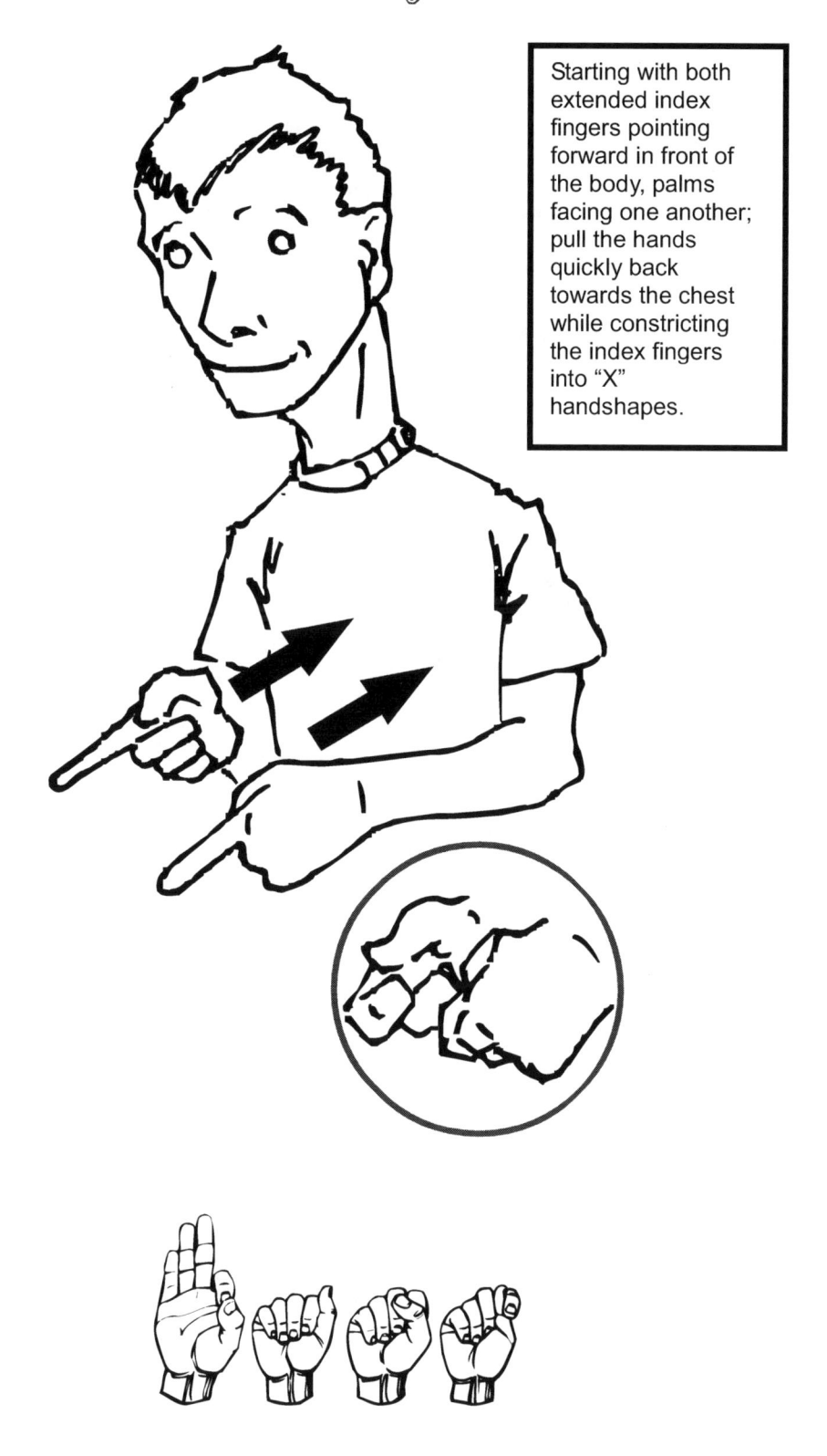

Starting with both extended index fingers pointing forward in front of the body, palms facing one another; pull the hands quickly back towards the chest while constricting the index fingers into "X" handshapes.

fast - rápido

Sports, Recreation, & Arts

Move the fingertips of the dominant "F" handshape, palm facing down, in a circular motion along the length of the back of the "S" reference handshape, held across the body and palm facing down.

field – terreno

Sports, Recreation, & Arts

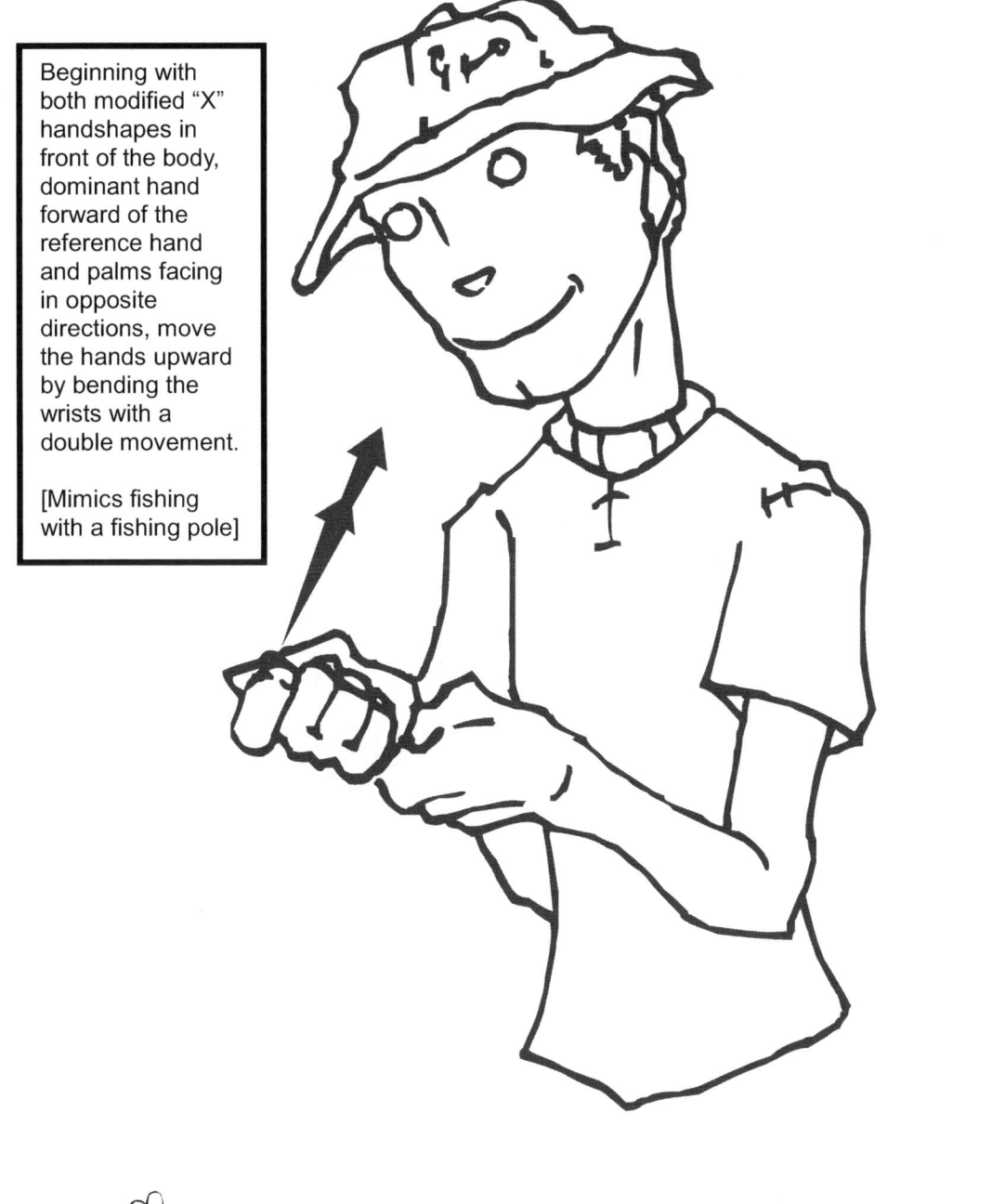

Beginning with both modified "X" handshapes in front of the body, dominant hand forward of the reference hand and palms facing in opposite directions, move the hands upward by bending the wrists with a double movement.

[Mimics fishing with a fishing pole]

fishing – pesca

Sports, Recreation, & Arts

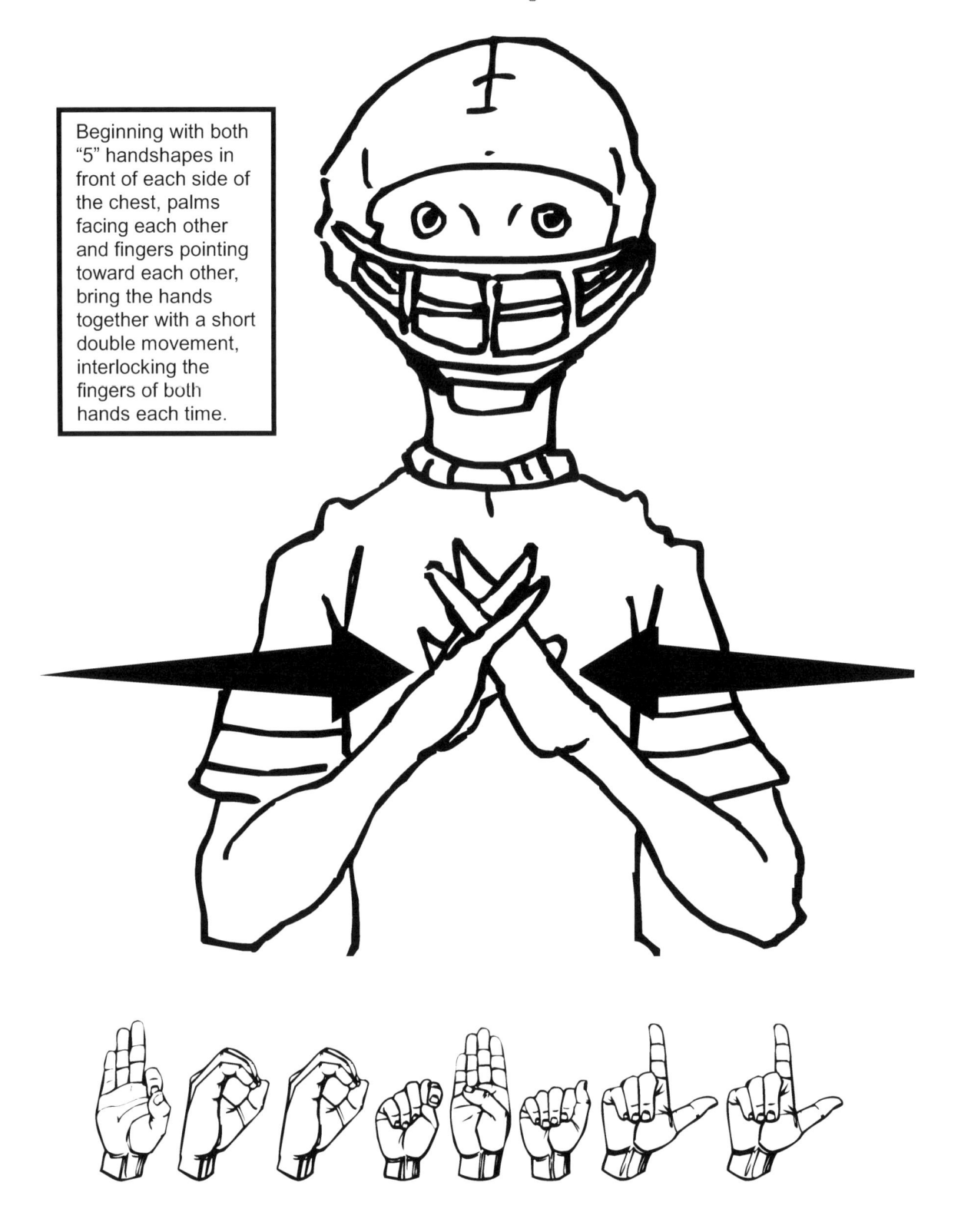

Beginning with both "5" handshapes in front of each side of the chest, palms facing each other and fingers pointing toward each other, bring the hands together with a short double movement, interlocking the fingers of both hands each time.

football - fútbol

Sports, Recreation, & Arts 103

Bring the knuckles of both "10" handshapes against each other, palms facing the body, in a slightly upward motion.

[As if two people facing each other in competition.]

game – juego

Sports, Recreation, & Arts

Beginning with the dominant modified "X" handshape near the dominant hip, palm facing reference side, and the reference modified "X" handshape in front of the dominant side of the body, palm facing in, swing the dominant hand upward and to the reference side.

[Mimics swinging a golf club]

golf - golf

Sports, Recreation, & Arts 105

Beginning with the modified "X" handshapes in front of each shoulder, palms facing each other, move the hands forward in small double circles by moving the arms and the wrists.

gymnasium - gimnasio

Sports, Recreation, & Arts

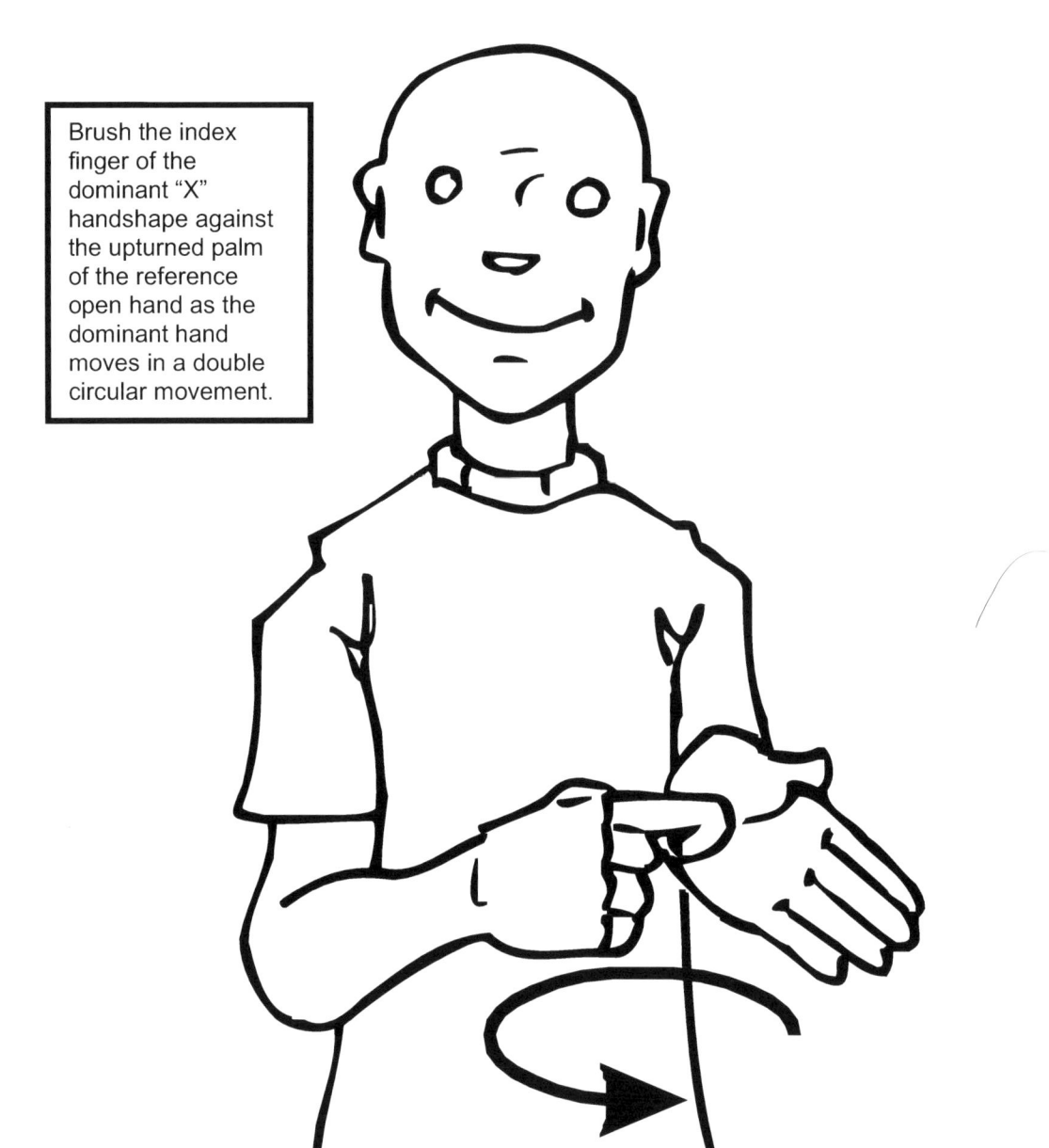

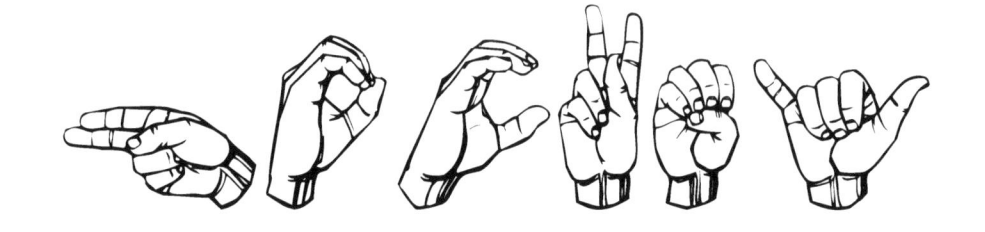

Brush the index finger of the dominant "X" handshape against the upturned palm of the reference open hand as the dominant hand moves in a double circular movement.

hockey - hockey

Sports, Recreation, & Arts

Begin with the extended thumb of the dominant "U" handshape against the dominant side of the forehead, palm facing forward, bend the fingers of the "U" handshape up and down with a double movement. Then move the dominant hand down into the "3" handshape onto the reference "B" handshape, with the reference hand between the middle and index finger of the dominant hand, move both forward a short distance.

horseback riding – montar a caballo

108   **Sports, Recreation, & Arts**

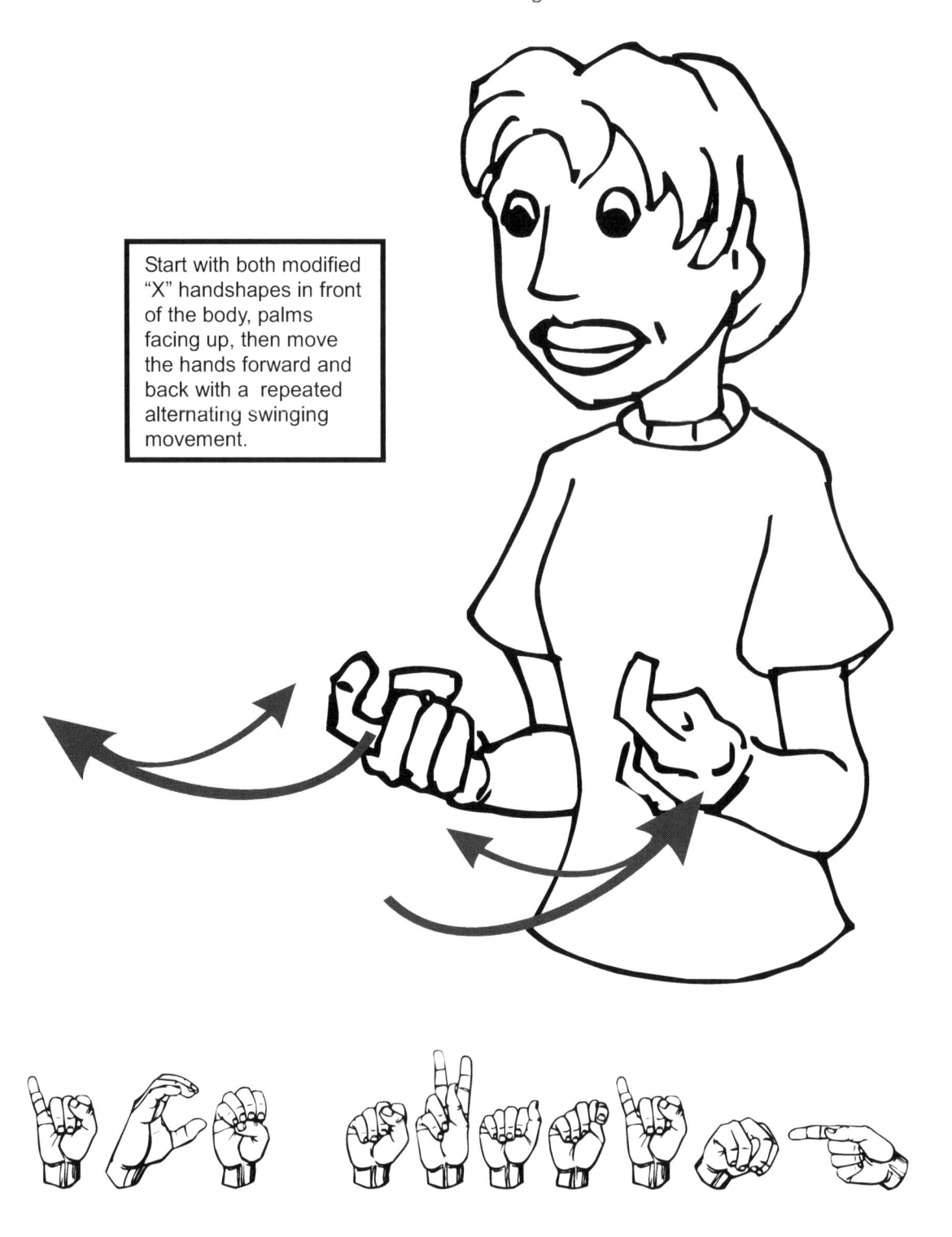

Start with both modified "X" handshapes in front of the body, palms facing up, then move the hands forward and back with a repeated alternating swinging movement.

ice skating – patinar sobre hielo

Sports, Recreation, & Arts109

> Place the dominant "V" handshape in a standing position on the reference palm; lift the "V" handshape, bending the knuckles, and return to a standing position.
>
> [Showing a jumping motion with your fingers]

jump – saltar

Sports, Recreation, & Arts

> Move the dominant "B" handshape upward in front of the body to hit the index finger side of the dominant hand against the little finger side of the reference "B" handshape with a single movement, both palms angled in.

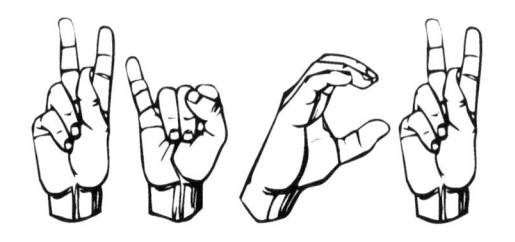

kick – patear

Sports, Recreation, & Arts 111

> Bring the palm side of the dominant "V" handshape, palm facing forward, from the shoulder downward to land on the upturned palm of the reference hand in front of the body.

lose – perder

Beginning with the index fingers and thumbs of both "F" handshapes intersecting in front of the reference side of the chest, palms facing each other and the dominant hand above the reference hand, release the fingers, flip the hands in reverse positions, and connect the fingers again with a repeated alternating movement as the hands move across the front of the body from reference to dominant side.

[Shows the Olympic rings chained together]

Olympics – Olímpico

Sports, Recreation, & Arts

113

Begin with the dominant curved "5" handshape, palm facing down, over the extended dominant index finger, palm facing dominant side and finger pointing up, in front of the body, move the hands down in a wavy movement.

[This represents the shape of a parachute and a person]

parachute – paracaídas

Sports, Recreation, & Arts

Swing both "Y" handshapes up and down by twisting the wrists in front of each side of the body with a repeated movement.

[Play as in recreation]

play – juego

Sports, Recreation, & Arts 115

> Rub the knuckles of the dominant "A" handshape, palm facing down, back and forth on the extended reference index finger held in front of the chest, palm facing down and finger pointing to dominant side, with repeated movements.

practice – practicar

116

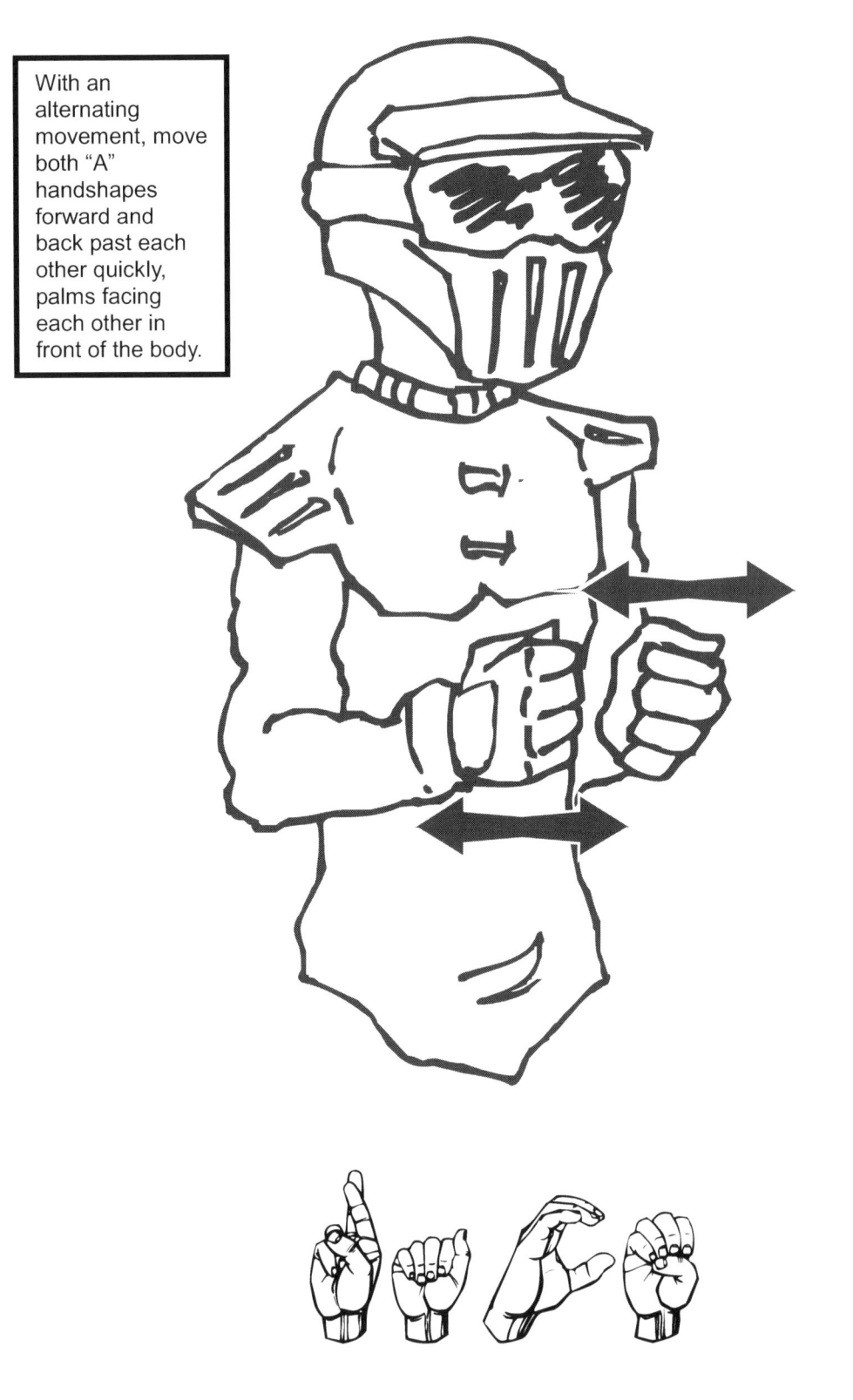

Sports, Recreation, & Arts

With an alternating movement, move both "A" handshapes forward and back past each other quickly, palms facing each other in front of the body.

race – carrera

Copyright © 2005 Time to Sign, Inc.

Sports, Recreation, & Arts   117

> Tap the fingertips of the dominant bent "V" handshape, palm facing in, against the lips with a double movement.
>
> [Also: whistle]

referee – árbitro

Tap the back of the dominant "S" handshape, palm facing up, on the back of the reference "S" handshape held in front of the chest, palm facing down, with a repeated movement. Then with both curved "5" handshapes in front of the chest, palms facing forward and the dominant hand higher than the reference hand, move the hands upward one at a time with an alternating movement.

rockclimb – escalar en roca

Sports, Recreation, & Arts — 119

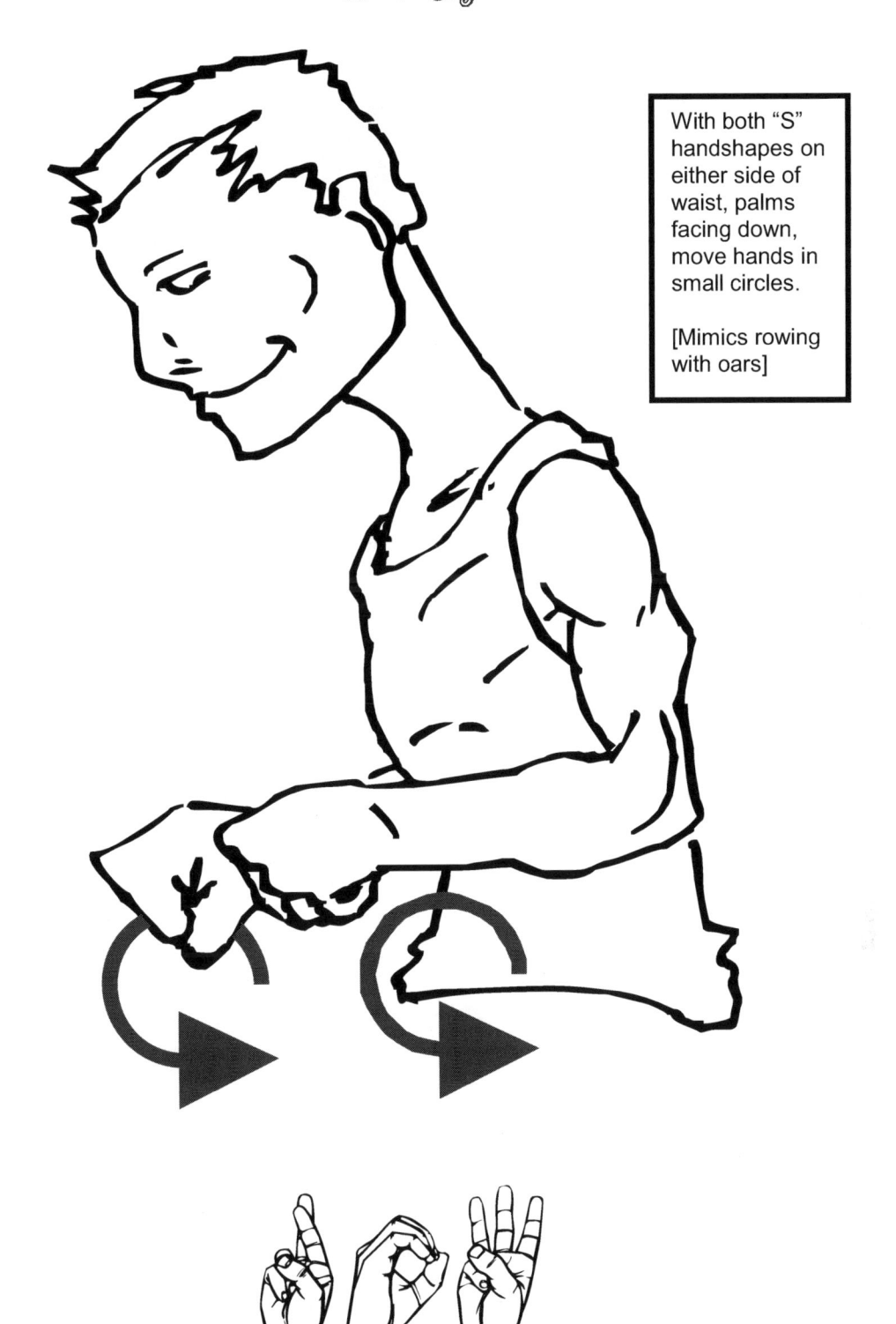

> With both "S" handshapes on either side of waist, palms facing down, move hands in small circles.
>
> [Mimics rowing with oars]

row – remar

120 Sports, Recreation, & Arts

Hook the index of the dominant "L" under the thumb of the reference "L" and move the hands forward in a quick short motion.

run - correr

Copyright © 2005 Time to Sign, Inc.

Sports, Recreation, & Arts 121

Beginning with the little finger side of the dominant "B" handshape, palm facing in, against the palm side of the reference "3" handshape, palm facing dominant side, move both hands forward a short distance.

sailing – navegar

Copyright © 2005-2013 Time to Sign, Inc.

122   Sports, Recreation, & Arts

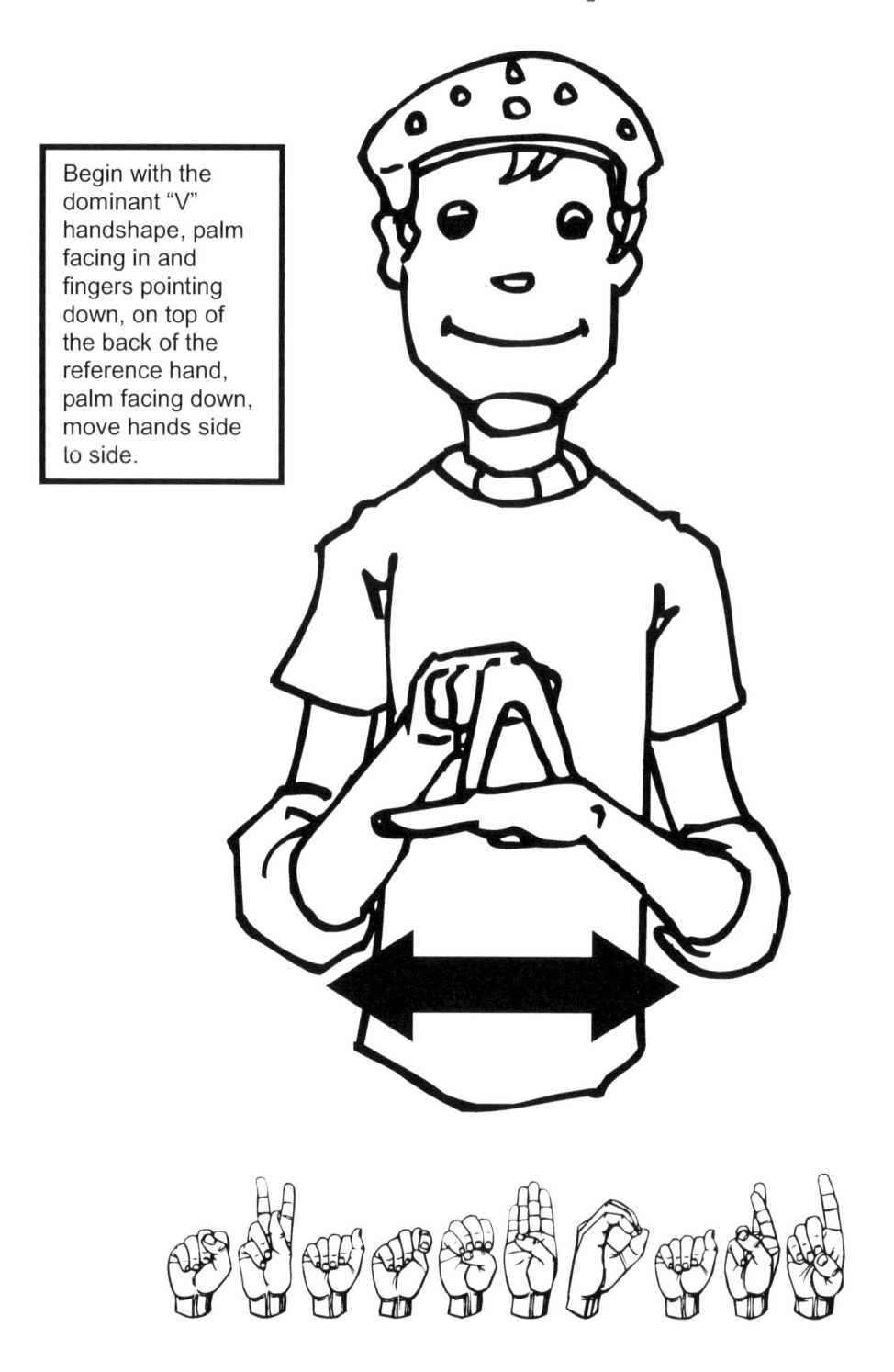

Begin with the dominant "V" handshape, palm facing in and fingers pointing down, on top of the back of the reference hand, palm facing down, move hands side to side.

skateboard – monopatín

Sports, Recreation, & Arts 123

Bring the dominant curved hand from over the reference side of the head, palm facing down, in a large arc to the dominant, ending above the dominant shoulder. Then with the palms of both open hands together in front of the chest, fingers pointing up, move the hands forward and downward in a large arc. Next, with the dominant curved "5" handshape, palm facing down, over the extended dominant index finger, palm facing dominant side, and fingers pointing up, in front of the dominant side of the body, move the hands to the reference side of the chest and then outward in an arc back to the dominant side of the chest.

[Sign: sky + dive + parachute]

skydiving–paracaidismo

Sports, Recreation, & Arts

Move the dominant "B" handshape upward in front of the body to hit the index finger side of the dominant hand against the little finger side of the reference "B" handshape with a double movement, both palms angled in.

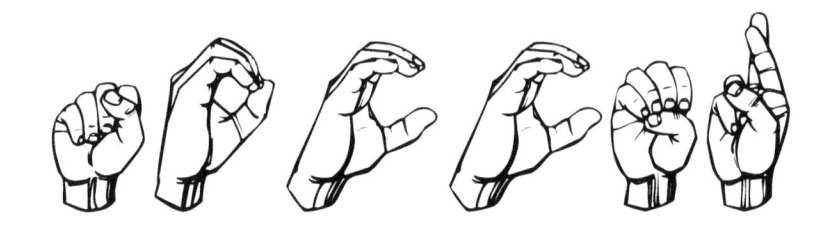

soccer – balonpié

Sports, Recreation, & Arts 125

> Bring the knuckles of both "10" handshapes against each other, palms facing the body, in a slightly upward motion with a double movement.
>
> [As if two people facing each other in competition.]

sports – deportes

126 — Sports, Recreation, & Arts

Move the dominant open hand, palm facing in, across the forehead and then shake the hand once in front of the dominant shoulder.

[Shows wiping sweat off of the forehead]

sweat - sudar

Sports, Recreation, & Arts — 127

Beginning with the fingers of both open hands crossed in front of the chest, palms facing down, move the hands apart to each side with a double movement.

[Demonstrates the movements of hands while swimming]

swimming – nadar

Copyright © 2005-2013 Time to Sign, Inc.

Sports, Recreation, & Arts

Beginning with the index fingers of both "T" handshapes touching on front of chest, palms angled forward, bring the hands away from each other in outward arcs while turning the palms in, ending with the little fingers touching.

team – equipo

Sports, Recreation, & Arts 129

Begin with the dominant "A" handshape, palm facing out, held to side of chest, bring the arm downward in an arc to waist and then back again.

[Mimics swinging a tennis racquet]

tennis – tenis

Sports, Recreation, & Arts

Beginning with the dominant "S" hand in front of the dominant shoulder, move the hand forward and downward while opening into a "5" handshape.

[Mimics throwing something.]

throw – tirar

Sports, Recreation, & Arts 131

Hook the index of the dominant "L" under the thumb of the reference "L" and move the hands forward in a quick short motion. Then with an alternating movement, move both "A" handshapes forward and back past each other quickly, palms facing each other in front of the body.

[Sign: run + race]

track – pista

Beginning with both open hands near each side of the head, palms facing forward and fingers pointing up, push the hands upward and forward with a double movement.

[Mimics hitting a volleyball]

volleyball – voleibol

Sports, Recreation, & Arts   133

Open hands, palms down, are moved in a forward-downward motion alternately in front of the body.

[As if walking with the hands.]

walk – andar, caminar

Beginning with dominant "5" handshape in front of the dominant shoulder, palm facing forward and fingers pointing up, and the reference "5" handshape in front of body, palm facing dominant side, sweep the dominant hand downward in an arc across the index-finger side of the reference hand while changing both hands into "S" handshapes and bringing the dominant hand upward in front of the chest.

win – ganar

SIGN LANGUAGE HANDOUT – FINE & PERFORMING ARTS

acting - actuación

art - arte

dance – bailar

draw - dibujar

paint – pintar

music - música

Sports, Recreation, & Arts 137

SIGN LANGUAGE HANDOUT - MUSIC

drum - tambor

guitar - guitarra

horn – trompeta

piano - piano

violin - violín

xylophone - xilófono

Copyright © 2005-2013 Time to Sign, Inc.

SIGN LANGUAGE HANDOUT – SPORTS & RECREATION

golf – golf

horseback riding – montar a caballo

ice skating – pantinar sobre hielo

swimming - nadar

tennis - tenis

sports - deportes

Sports, Recreation, & Arts   139

SIGN LANGUAGE HANDOUT
TEAM SPORTS

baseball - béisbol

basketball - baloncesto

football - fútbol

hockey - hockey

soccer - balonpie

team - equipo

Copyright © 2005-2013 Time to Sign, Inc.

SIGN LANGUAGE HANDOUT - SPORTS & RECREATION

ball - pelota

game – juego

camp - acampar

practice - practicar

lose - perder

win – ganar

Index

— A —

Acting.............................51
Art..................................52
Audience.......................53

— B —

Backpack......................83
Ball.................................84
Band..............................54
Baseball........................85
Basket...........................55
Basketball....................86
Beauty...........................56
Bicycle..........................87
Boat...............................88
Bow................................57
Boxing...........................89

— C —

Camera.........................58
Camp.............................90
Captain.........................91
Car.................................92
Catch.............................93
Champion.....................94
Cheer.............................95
Climbing.......................96
Competition.................97
Crayon..........................59
Culture Art...................60

— D —

Dance............................61
Dive................................98
Draw..............................62
Drum..............................63

— F —

Fast................................99
Field.............................100
Fine Art.........................64

Fishing........................101
Football......................102

— G —

Game...........................103
Glue...............................65
Golf..............................104
Guitar............................66
Gymnasium................105

— H —

Hockey........................106
Horn...............................67
Horseback Riding.....107

— I —

Ice Skating.................108

— J —

Jump............................109

— K —

Kick..............................110

— L —

Lose.............................111

— M —

Music.............................68

— O —

Olympics.....................112

— P —

Paint..............................69
Paper.............................70
Parachute...................113
Performing Art............71
Piano.............................72
Picture..........................73
Play.............................114

Practice......................115
Puppet..........................74

— R —

Racing.........................116
Referee.......................117
Rock Climb................118
Row..............................119
Run..............................120

— S —

Sailing.........................121
Scissors.......................75
Skateboard................122
Skydiving...................123
Smooth.........................76
Soccer........................124
Sports.........................125
Statue...........................77
Sweat..........................126
Swimming...................127

— T —

Talent............................78
Team...........................128
Tennis.........................129
Texture.........................79
Throw..........................130
Track...........................131

— V —

Violin.............................80
Volleyball...................132

— W —

Walk............................133
Win..............................134

— X —

Xylophone....................81

Copyright © 2005 Time to Sign, Inc.

CHECK OUT OUR GREAT PRODUCTS AT WWW.TIMETOSIGN.COM

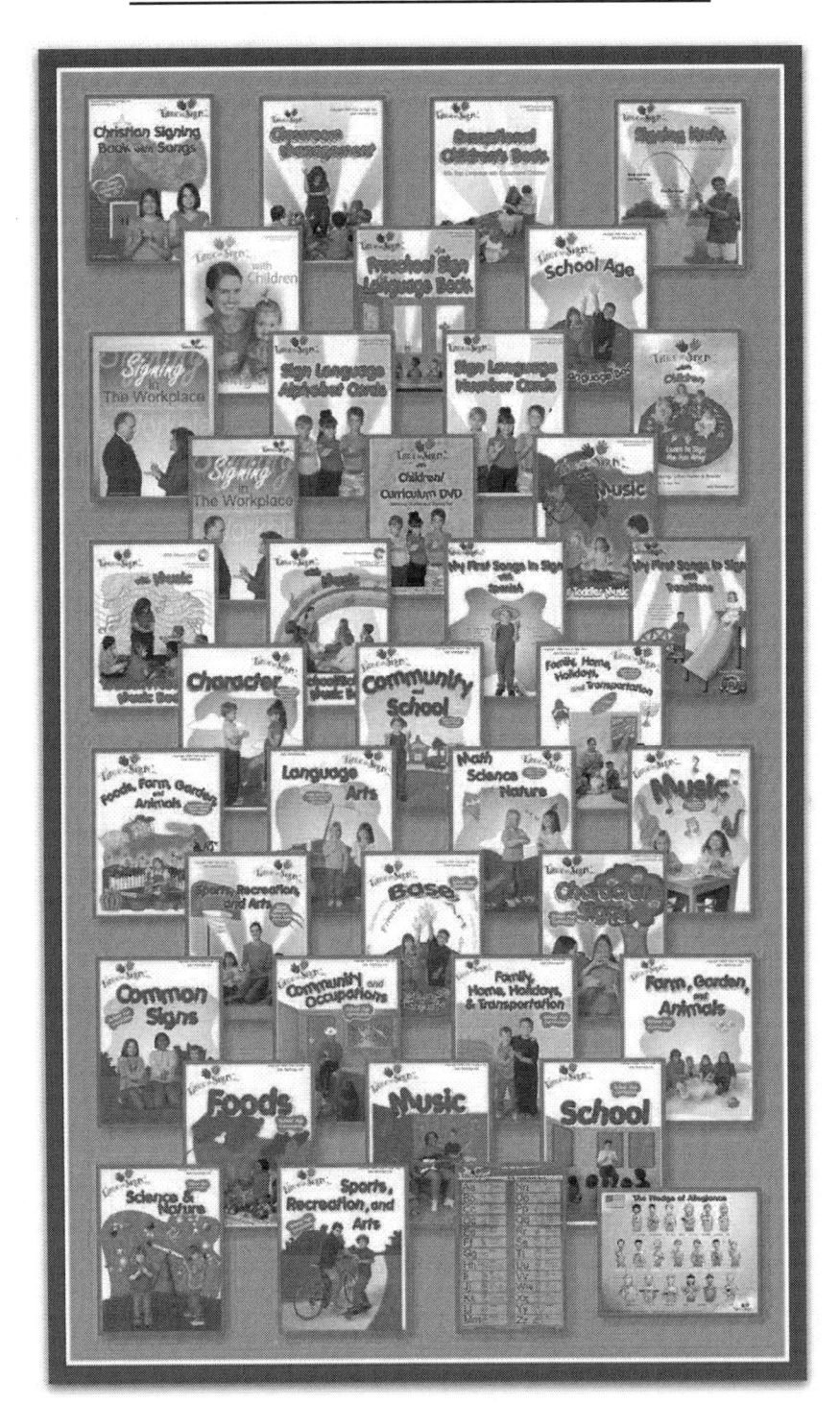

MICHAEL & LILLIAN HUBLER

ABOUT THE AUTHORS

Michael and Lillian Hubler founded Time to Sign, Inc. in 2000. The company was founded because the Hublers recognized the benefits of using American Sign Language (ASL) with their children; and then to other children, families, educators, and care givers around the world. Time to Sign programs have been used in Family Childcares, Private Preschools, Early Head Start, Head Start, and School Districts.

Lillian is a nationally acclaimed presenter/trainer. Since 2000, she has trained over 50,000 educators, parents and children around the world in age appropriate and developmentally appropriate sign language usage. She is renowned for her high energy workshops and presentations. She has appeared on CNN, ABC, NBC, as we'll as interviewed by Florida Today and the Washington Post.

Michael is Director of Educational Curriculum and Product Development for Time to Sign. He is currently working on his doctorate dissertation in the field of education, specializing in the positive impacts of sign language on social and emotional development. Michael has served as an executive director for various educational and community services organizations, specializing in services and programs to enhance the education, personal growth, and development of at-risk children.

Michael and Lillian also owned a licensed day care with 135 children from birth to 12 years of age. They have written over 25 sign language books including preschool and school-age curriculums. Time to Sign's trainings and materials are uniquely designed to promote social emotional development and reduce children's challenging behavior in social settings. Their training programs and materials also promote literacy, language development, and communication.

Made in the USA
Columbia, SC
01 October 2023